P9-EMK-889

Michael A. Covington., Ph.D.,
Associate Research Scientist,
Artificial Intelligence Program
University of Georgia

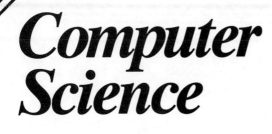
Computer Science

BARRON'S

SOLI DEO GLORIA

All inquiries should be addressed to:
Barron's Educational Series, Inc.
250 Wireless Boulevard
Hauppauge, New York 11788

Library of Congress Catalog Card No. 90-23549

International Standard Book No. 0-8120-4586-6

Library of Congress Cataloging-in-Publication Data
Covington, Michael.
   Study keys to computer science / Michael A. Covington.
      p.   cm.—(Barron's study keys)
   Includes index.
   ISBN 0-8120-4586-6
   1. Computer science—Study and teaching.   I. Title.   II.
Series.
QA76.27.C74   1991   90-23549
004'.071'173—dc20   CIP

PRINTED IN THE UNITED STATES OF AMERICA

1234   5500   98765432

CONTENTS

To the reader

This book is for computer science students who want to review their course material quickly.

The book is divided into short chapters called **Keys,** grouped into units called **Themes.** Each Theme begins with an overview of one area of computer science.

Unlike other fields, computer science does not normally begin with a "survey course." Thus there is no course that covers everything in this book. Parts of this book are sure to be unfamiliar to you. Make the most of what interests you or corresponds to the course you have taken.

You don't have to take the sections in the order in which they're printed, either; feel free to skip around.

The **computer programs** in this book are written in Turbo Pascal 5.5 unless otherwise noted. They were written to be **understandable, not efficient**. They are designed to help you understand how computations are done; they are not always designed for use "as is" on the computer. Sometimes they leave out declarations or other necessary material.

I want to thank numerous colleagues for help with this book (especially Doug Downing, Don Potter, Dan Everett, Jim Koehler, and Jeff Prosise); my daughters Sharon and Cathy, who put up with a certain lack of "daddy time" this summer; and especially my wife Melody, who prodded me to buy a laptop computer without which the book would not have been finished on time.

University of Georgia   Michael A. Covington
September 1990

Theme 1   HOW COMPUTERS WORK

*C*omputer science is the study of the general principles that hold true for many or all computers, rather than the arbitrary details involved in using a particular program. This Theme deals with how computers work on the most basic level. Modern computers are *digital,* which means they represent information with two kinds of electrical signals, called "on" and "off," "1" and "0," or "true" and "false." Each signal of this kind is called a *bit,* and combinations of bits represent numbers and printed characters. The main parts of a computer are the central processing unit (CPU), memory, and input-output devices. A *program,* stored in the computer, tells the CPU what to do.

INDIVIDUAL KEYS IN THIS THEME
1   How computers work
2   Parts of a computer
3   Micro-, mini-, and mainframe computers
4   Bit patterns: binary, hex, octal
5   Character sets
6   CPU and bus
7   CPU architectures

Key 1 How computers work

OVERVIEW *Almost all modern computers use **Von Neumann** architecture. This means that the computer consists of a **central processing unit (CPU)** together with **memory**, plus **input-output (i-o) devices** such as screen, keyboard, and printer.*

The CPU: All computation goes on in the **central processing unit (CPU)**, which controls the rest of the computer.
- The CPU is controlled by a **program** consisting of **instruction codes** stored in memory.
- Memory also contains the **data** (information) that the computer is to work on.

Bits: All the contents of memory—instructions as well as data—consist of groups of **bits**. A **bit** is a signal with two possible values, called "on" and "off," "true" and "false," or "1" and "0."

Bytes: Most computer memories store bits in groups of 8, called **bytes**. Sometimes they use larger groups called **words**.

Binary number: We can interpret any series of bits as a **binary (base-2) number**. Computers do arithmetic on bit patterns by interpreting them as numbers in this way.

Characters: Groups of bits can also stand for letters, digits, etc., one byte per character. Most computers use the **ASCII character set** (American Standard Code for Information Interchange).

The bus: The CPU communicates with memory and i-o devices via the **bus**, which is a system of parallel connections.
- Each memory location and i-o device recognizes a unique **address** that can be placed on address lines of the bus to identify it.
- Each address is simply a bit pattern.

KEY EXAMPLE

To store bit pattern 00011100 at location 00000001, the computer places the address 00000001 on the address part of the bus and the value 00011100 on the data part of the bus.

Key 2 Parts of a computer

OVERVIEW *When we say "computer," we almost always mean a* **digital** *computer with* **Von Neumann architecture.**

Digital computers: Digital means that the computer represents all information (**data**) in the form of **bits**, electrical signals that are either "on" or "off" with no value in between. (A computer with more than two values would still be digital, provided the values were sharply distinct.)

Von Neumann architecture: Von Neumann architecture (invented by John Von Neumann, 1903-1957) means that the actions of the computer are controlled by a **program** stored in memory. Programs are called **software** and are distinct from the machine itself (**hardware**).

KEY PARTS OF A COMPUTER

Memory: Where data and instructions are stored while being processed.
- **ROM (read-only memory)** is permanently recorded and cannot be changed; ROM contains instructions that control the computer when it is first turned on.
- **RAM (random-access memory)** contains all other instructions and data; on most computers RAM goes blank when the computer is turned off.

Input-output (i-o) devices: Keyboard, screen, printer, disk drives, etc., that enable the computer to communicate with the outside world and to store information permanently.

The central processing unit (CPU): Spends its time reading instruction codes from memory and obeying (**executing**) them.

Key 3 Micro-, mini-, and mainframe computers

OVERVIEW *Computers are classified as **mainframe**, **minicomputer**, or **microcomputer**. (See Keys 13-14 on supercomputers.)*

Mainframe computers: Complete computer fills a room; CPU is the size of a refrigerator. The word "mainframe" also refers to the cabinet or frame in which the parts of the CPU are mounted. *Examples:* IBM 370, IBM 3090, CDC CYBER, largest models of Digital Equipment Corporation VAX.

- Mainframe computers are big enough for the largest businesses and research institutions.
- Hundreds of people at **terminals** can use a mainframe computer at once. A terminal is a screen plus a keyboard.

Minicomputers: CPU fits on one or two printed circuit boards; whole machine fits into one large box. Adequate for a medium-sized business or a single university department. *Examples:* IBM AS/400, Digital Equipment Corporation VAX (most models), Data General Eclipse.

Microcomputers: Entire CPU on a single chip of silicon. Such a CPU is called a **microprocessor** and is a type of **integrated circuit (IC)**.

- ICs are made by putting different impurities in different places on the same chip of silicon, so that it becomes a whole set of interconnected components (transistors, diodes, resistors, etc.).
- Early microcomputers: Apple II, TRS-80 Model 1, Commodore PET (all introduced 1977).
- **IBM PC** (1981) was the first microcomputer widely used in business and industry; compatible machines from other makers **(clones)** immediately appeared on the market.
- **Supermicros (workstations)** such as NeXT, Sun Sparcstation, IBM 6000 are as powerful as the mainframes of a few years earlier.

Key 4 Bit patterns: binary, hex, and octal

OVERVIEW *Computers represent all information as bits (Key 2). Bit patterns can be interpreted as numbers.*

Binary and hex numbers: Any series of bits can be interpreted as a **binary (base-2) number**. In binary, the only digits are 0 and 1, and instead of 1s, 10s, and 100s, the columnar positions stand for 1s, 2s, 4s, 8s, etc.

Hex numbers: Computer programmers also use **hexadecimal ("hex") (base-16)** numbers, in which the digits are 0, 1, 2, 3, 4, 5, 6, 7, 8, 9, A, B, C, D, E, F, and the columns stand for 1s, 16s, 256s, etc.

KEY EXAMPLE

The number 230 represented 3 ways

128s
  64s
    32s
      16s
        8s
          4s   100s
            2s   16s   10s
              1s   1s   1s

1 1 1 0 0 1 1 1	=	E 6	=	2 3 0
Binary (Base 2)		Hexadecimal (Base 16)		Decimal (Base 10)

Hex as abbreviations for binary: Each **hex digit** corresponds to **4 binary digits**.

E = 1110, 6 = 0110, so E6 = 11100110.

Translating binary to hex is much easier than binary to decimal. You can take digits in groups of 4, without looking at the entire number. This makes hex a handy way of abbreviating binary numbers.

- On some computers, **octal** (base 8) numbers are used to abbreviate binary numbers by taking digits in groups of 3 instead of 4.

Key 5 Character sets

OVERVIEW *To use keyboards, screens, and printers, the computer represents each character as a bit pattern. ASCII code is a common way of representing each character with 8 bits.*

ASCII character set (American Standard Code for Information Interchange): In ASCII, bit pattern 01000001 (hex 41) represents A, 00100010 (hex 42) represents B, and so forth. (See Table 1.)
- Codes for the digits 0-9 are **not** the numbers 0 to 9.
- ASCII codes 0-31 and 127 are **control codes**, not printable characters.
- Not all control codes have agreed-upon meanings.
- Ctrl-L ("form feed") usually makes a printer start a new page.
- Ctrl-S usually makes the computer stop sending information to the terminal, and Ctrl-Q makes it resume.

Other character sets: Some of these are variations of ASCII; others are very different. For example:
- The **IBM PC character set** consists of ASCII plus additional codes in the range 128-255. For example, 137 is ë, 247 is ≈. This includes **box-drawing characters** such as:

    218 ⌐ 191 ⌐ 196 − 179 | 197 + 192 ∟ 217 ⌐
- IBM mainframes use the **EBCDIC character set** (Extended Binary-Coded Decimal Interchange Code); this works like ASCII but uses different codes and makes it easier to convert digits to numbers.
- Character sets for **foreign languages** have been developed. In Chinese and Japanese, two bytes are used for each character; this allows 65,536 different codes.

TABLE 1.

ASCII character set

Decimal	Hex	How typed	Decimal	Hex	Character							
0	0	Ctrl-@	32	20	Space	64	40	@	96	60	'
1	1	Ctrl-A	33	21	!	65	41	A	97	61	a
2	2	Ctrl-B	34	22	"	66	42	B	98	62	b
3	3	Ctrl-C	35	23	#	67	43	C	99	63	c
4	4	Ctrl-D	36	24	$	68	44	D	100	64	d
5	5	Ctrl-E	37	25	%	69	45	E	101	65	e
6	6	Ctrl-F	38	26	&	70	46	F	102	66	f
7	7	Ctrl-G	39	27	'	71	47	G	103	67	g
8	8	Ctrl-H	40	28	(	72	48	H	104	68	h
9	9	Tab	41	29	)	73	49	I	105	69	i
10	A	Ctrl-J	42	2A	*	74	4A	J	106	6A	j
11	B	Ctrl-K	43	2B	+	75	4B	K	107	6B	k
12	C	Ctrl-L	44	2C	,	76	4C	L	108	6C	l
13	D	Return	45	2D	−	77	4D	M	109	6D	m
14	E	Ctrl-N	46	2E	.	78	4E	N	110	6E	n
15	F	Ctrl-O	47	2F	/	79	4F	O	111	6F	o
16	10	Ctrl-P	48	30	0	80	50	P	112	70	p
17	11	Ctrl-Q	49	31	1	81	51	Q	113	71	q
18	12	Ctrl-R	50	32	2	82	52	R	114	72	r
19	13	Ctrl-S	51	33	3	83	53	S	115	73	s
20	14	Ctrl-T	52	34	4	84	54	T	116	74	t
21	15	Ctrl-U	53	35	5	85	55	U	117	75	u
22	16	Ctrl-V	54	36	6	86	56	V	118	76	v
23	17	Ctrl-W	55	37	7	87	57	W	119	77	w
24	18	Ctrl-X	56	38	8	88	58	X	120	78	x
25	19	Ctrl-Y	57	39	9	89	59	Y	121	79	y
26	1A	Ctrl-Z	58	3A	:	90	5A	Z	122	7A	z
27	1B	Escape	59	3B	;	91	5B	[	123	7B	{
28	1C	Ctrl-\	60	3C	<	92	5C	\	124	7C	|
29	1D	Ctrl-]	61	3D	=	93	5D	]	125	7D	}
30	1E	Ctrl-^	62	3E	>	94	5E	^	126	7E	~
31	1F	Ctrl-_	63	3F	?	95	5F	_	127	7F	Delete

Key 6 CPU and bus

OVERVIEW *The CPU communicates with the rest of the computer via the **bus**, a system of parallel connections.*

Inside the CPU: The CPU (**central processing unit**) of a computer contains **functional units**, which are circuits that perform operations (add, subtract, compare, shift, store, etc.), and **registers**, which are places data can be held temporarily.

Words: The amount of data that a register can hold is called a **word**; for example, a "16-bit" CPU has registers that hold 16 bits each.

The bus: The CPU communicates with memory and with input-output devices via the **bus**, a system of parallel wires or connections that makes it possible to connect all parts of the computer in parallel, rather than connecting each of them separately to each of the others.

Using the bus for communication: Each memory location holds one **byte** (8 bits) and has a unique **address** (a bit pattern that identifies the location, regardless of what is stored there). (Some computers assign addresses to words rather than bytes.)

- The bus consists of **data lines, address lines,** and a few lines for **control signals** (Figure 1).
- **To read a byte** from memory, the CPU places the address on the address lines (one bit on each address line), then puts a 1 on the "Read Memory" line. Memory responds by retrieving the byte from that address and placing it on the data lines (one bit on each data line), from which the CPU can obtain it.
- **To store a byte** into memory, the CPU places the address on the address lines and the data on the data lines, then places a 1 on the "Write Memory" line. Memory accepts the byte and stores it at the specified address.

FIGURE 1

The bus is a system of parallel wires or connections that link the CPU to memory and input-output devices.

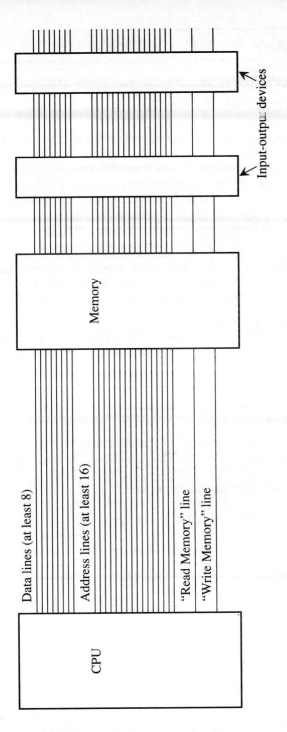

Key 7   CPU architectures

OVERVIEW   *The performance of a computer depends on the design of the CPU.*

Clock speed: The step-by-step operation of the CPU is controlled by an electrical signal called the **clock** that constantly switches back and forth from 0 to 1. The speed (frequency) of the clock is measured in **megahertz (MHz)** (millions of cycles per second).
- A 20-MHz CPU is twice as fast as a 10-MHz CPU—but only if they are otherwise identical in design.
- Most speed differences between computers come from differences in design, not differences in clock speed.

Registers: CPUs differ in the number of registers (temporary holding places for data; there are normally 4 to 16) and the number of bits in each (the **word length**, usually 8, 16, or 32).

Instruction set: All CPUs can do integer arithmetic and compare bit patterns, and do logical operations on bits (Key 9). Some CPUs can also do floating-point arithmetic, fast text searching, and other things. On simpler CPUs, the programmer has to construct these operations out of simpler operations that the CPU provides.

RISC vs. CISC

A **complex instruction set computer (CISC)** has many operations built in, most or all of which take more than one clock cycle. *Examples:* IBM 370, IBM 3090, DEC VAX, almost all microcomputers. A **reduced instruction set computer (RISC)** has fewer operations built in, but each operation takes only one clock cycle. *Examples:* Sun Sparcstation, IBM 6000. **RISC is faster** if memory is relatively fast, so that no time is wasted fetching the instructions. **CISC is faster** if memory is relatively slow, because the same work can be done without fetching as many instruction codes.

Theme 2 COMPUTER ARCHITECTURE

*C*omputer architecture is the study of how computers are designed and built. The CPU of a computer is made of logic circuits, which are simple electronic circuits that operate on bits. Modern computers get their versatility from the fact that they are controlled by programs stored in memory. Alongside conventional digital computers, there are several other types, including supercomputers and parallel computers.

Key 8 Logic circuits

OVERVIEW *Computers rely on the fact that a* **transistor**
*conducts electricity in one place when a voltage is applied in
another place. Thus a signal in one place can produce a
signal (the same or different) in another place.*

Transistors: A **transistor** conducts electricity when a signal is applied
to its input. (Some early computers achieved this effect with electro-
magnets flipping switches. Slightly later computers used vacuum
tubes.)
- The field-effect transistor in Figure 2A conducts when its input is
  + 5 volts but not when its input is 0 volts.
- When the transistor is conducting, the output is 0 volts because the
  transistor provides a path from output to ground (0 V). But when
  the transistor is not conducting, the output is + 5 V through the
  resistor.

NOT gates: This circuit is called a **NOT gate**. Let + 5 volts represent
binary 1, and let 0 volts represent binary 0. Then the NOT gate turns
any bit into its opposite: its output is 1 when the input is 0, and vice
versa. This is called the logical NOT operation.

NOR gates: Figure 2B shows a **NOR gate**. Its output is 0 whenever at
least one of the inputs is 1 (because the output is connected to ground
whenever at least one transistor is conducting). Alongside the NOR
gate is shown its **truth table**.

Other gates: NOR and NOT gates can be combined to build other gates.
Figure 2C shows AND, OR, and NAND gates with their **truth
tables**. These truth tables are just like those used in **formal logic
(Boolean algebra)**, and every logic circuit is the implementation of a
logical formula.

Decoders: Also shown is a **decoder**, a circuit that recognizes a particular
bit pattern. CPUs use decoders to recognize instruction codes.

Key 9 From logic gates to CPU

OVERVIEW *Logic gates can do computations, such as adding numbers. Sequential logic circuits such as flip-flops can store data temporarily. A CPU consists of **functional units** such as adder, multiplier, etc. (made of gates), **decoders** (Key 8) to recognize instruction codes, and **registers** (made of flip-flops) to hold data.*

Arithmetic: Logic gates (**combinatorial logic circuits**) can do computations. Gates can be built with appropriate truth tables to do subtraction, comparison, and other operations.

- Figure 3A shows a gate called **full adder** that adds 3 one-digit binary numbers, together with its truth table. (A **half adder** adds only 2 numbers.)
- Figure 3B shows how to combine four 1-bit adders to make a **4-bit adder**. The same could be done for 8, 16, or any number of bits.
- The 4-bit adder adds only 2 numbers even though it is made of 3-input adders. The third input on each of the adders receives a digit **carried** from the previous adder. This is just like carrying in pencil-and-paper arithmetic.
- This 4-bit adder also detects **overflow**, what happens when a number is too large to fit in the available number of bits. *Example:* 1111 + 1111 = 11110, which is too big to fit into 4 bits. If the 4-bit adder performs this operation, its overflow-indicating output will be 1.

Sequential logic circuits: Unlike combinatorial circuits, these work through one operation after another, step by step.

Flip-flop: The basis of all sequential logic is the **flip-flop**, a logic circuit that can remember its previous state, shown in Figure 3C. The two inputs are called S (set) and R (reset).

KEY EXAMPLE: How a flip-flop works (Figure 3C)

If S = 0 and R = 0, the output is initially unpredictable. To ''set'' the flip-flop, let S = 1. Then Q becomes 0. Now let S drop back to 0, and Q will remain 0. But if you then ''reset'' the flip-flop by letting R = 1, Q will become 1 and will remain so after R drops back to 0. The flip-flop ''remembers.''

FIGURE 2

A. NOT gate

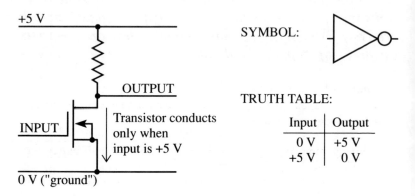

SYMBOL:

TRUTH TABLE:

Input	Output
0 V	+5 V
+5 V	0 V

B. NOR gate

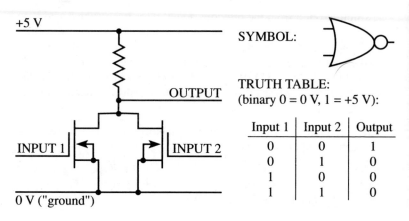

SYMBOL:

TRUTH TABLE:
(binary 0 = 0 V, 1 = +5 V):

Input 1	Input 2	Output
0	0	1
0	1	0
1	0	0
1	1	0

FIGURE 2 (continued)

C. Other gates made from NOR and NOT gates

OR gate:

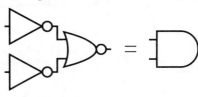

Input 1	Input 2	Output
0	0	0
0	1	1
1	0	1
1	1	1

AND gate:

Input 1	Input 2	Output
0	0	0
0	1	0
1	0	0
1	1	1

NAND gate:

Input 1	Input 2	Output
0	0	1
0	1	1
1	0	1
1	1	0

Decoder for bit pattern 0110
(a similar decoder could be built for any other bit pattern):

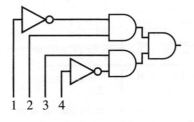

Input 1	Input 2	Input 3	Input 4	Output
0	1	1	0	1
All other combinations				0

FIGURE 3

A. 3–input 1–bit binary adder ("full adder")

Inputs			Outputs		Binary arithmetic
C	B	A	S1	S0	
0	0	0	0	0	0 + 0 + 0 = 0
0	0	1	0	1	0 + 0 + 1 = 1
0	1	0	0	1	0 + 1 + 0 = 1
0	1	1	1	0	0 + 1 + 1 = 10
1	0	0	0	1	1 + 0 + 0 = 1
1	0	1	1	0	1 + 0 + 1 = 10
1	1	0	1	0	1 + 1 + 0 = 10
1	1	1	1	1	1 + 1 + 1 = 11

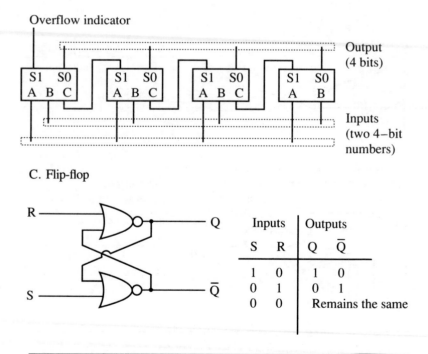

B. 4–bit adder made from 4 1–bit adders

Overflow indicator

Output (4 bits)

Inputs (two 4–bit numbers)

C. Flip-flop

Inputs		Outputs	
S	R	Q	$\overline{Q}$
1	0	1	0
0	1	0	1
0	0	Remains the same	

Key 10 Input and output from the CPU's viewpoint

OVERVIEW *The CPU uses the bus not only to communicate with memory, but also to communicate with input-output (i-o) devices.*

Memory-mapped i-o: The simplest way for the CPU to communicate with i-o devices is to use **memory-mapped i-o**, in which some memory addresses are set aside for i-o devices rather than real memory. *Example:* On the IBM PC, one way to display characters on the screen is simply to store them at memory addresses B0000 to B07CF (**video memory**).
- On some computers, data received from the keyboard or other devices automatically appears at certain memory addresses, ready for the CPU to read it.
- Memory-mapped i-o is fast, but it uses up addresses that could otherwise be used for ordinary memory.

Port addresses: The alternative is to assign **port addresses** to i-o devices. These work like memory addresses but do not refer to memory locations. The CPU reads or writes a port address by activating the "Read I-O" or "Write I-O" control line instead of "Read Memory" or "Write Memory."

Controllers: Many i-o devices have **controllers**, which are really special-purpose CPUs that execute instruction codes of their own. Rather than handling every detail of i-o by itself, the CPU can give instructions to the controllers.
- Disk drives, video screens, and serial communication ports usually have controllers.
- Disk drive controllers often have **direct memory access (DMA)**. This means, for example, that the CPU can tell the disk controller to copy a particular block of data from memory to disk, and the disk controller can obtain the data from memory without further help from the CPU.

FIGURE 4

Input-output devices on the bus are activated by the "Read I-O" and "Write I-O" control signals.

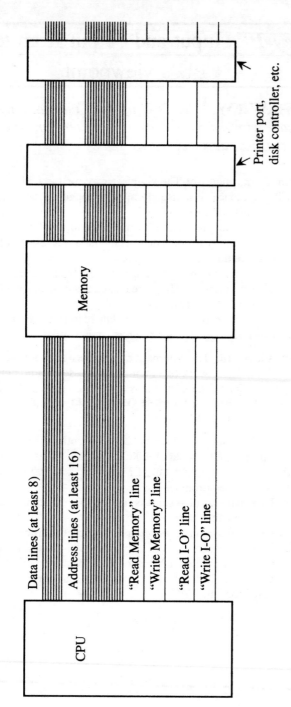

Data lines (at least 8)

Address lines (at least 16)

"Read Memory" line

"Write Memory" line

"Read I-O" line

"Write I-O" line

CPU

Memory

Printer port, disk controller, etc.

Key 11   Programming: Machine and assembly language

OVERVIEW   *A program is a series of instruction codes for the CPU to execute.*

KEY EXAMPLE

This program for the IBM PC wastes time for about half a second (a way to make the computer pause after writing information on the screen). The program stores 0000 in the AX register, keeps adding 1 until an overflow occurs, then terminates itself by returning control to the *operating system (Keys 15-23).*

Address	Instruction code (hex)	Assembly language	Explanation
0100	B8	MOV AX,0000	Store 0000 in AX register
0101	00		
0102	00		
0103	40	A: INC AX	Add 1 to AX register
0104	71	JNO A	If no overflow occurred,
0105	FD		jump to "A" (address 0103)
0106	CD	INT 20H	Call interrupt service routine 20 (terminate program)
0107	20		

Machine and assembly language: Instruction codes are referred to as **machine language**, but programmers normally use **assembly language**, a set of abbreviations (**mnemonics**) for instruction codes.

Assemblers: After writing a program in assembly language, the programmer runs a program called an **assembler** to translate it into the actual instruction codes, which can then be **loaded** into memory and executed.

Interrupts and system services: The last instruction in this program, INT 20H, is an **interrupt**. It tells the CPU to stop whatever it is doing, execute **interrupt service routine** number 20 (hex), and then resume where it left off.
  • On the PC, this is a way to get services from the operating system.
  • Other kinds of computers use interrupts only to deal with external events (keys pressed on the keyboard, etc.).
  • All CPUs have some way of **calling a subroutine** (executing codes that are stored elsewhere, then continuing with the main program). The PC itself has a CALL instruction distinct from INT.

Key 12 Programming: Compilers and interpreters

OVERVIEW *Instead of assembly language, most programs are written in **high-level programming languages** like BASIC, Pascal, or C. High-level languages allow programmers to express instructions in a notation that fits the work to be done, rather than in CPU instruction codes.*

Advantages of high-level languages:
- High-level languages are **portable**.
  A Pascal program will run, with little or no change, on any computer that has Pascal.
  A machine-language or assembly-language program will run only on the type of CPU for which it was written.
- High-level languages are **concise**.
  High-level languages allow the programmer to **express common operations simply** even if they are not simple for the CPU. *Example:* Finding a square root takes 50–100 lines of assembly language code, but in Pascal the programmer need only write sqrt.

How high-level languages are used:
- High-level languages **must be translated into machine language** in order for the program to run. This is done by a program called a **compiler**.
- An alternative is to use an **interpreter**, which does not produce a translation, but instead, reads the high-level-language program one step at a time and immediately does whatever the program says to do.

KEY EXAMPLE

Program from Key 11, rewritten in Pascal

Pascal language	*Explanation*
program demo;	Name of program is "demo"
var X: integer;	X will contain an integer (whole number)
begin	Beginning of instructions
X : = 0;	Store 0 in X
repeat	Repeat the following instruction:
X : = X + 1	Add 1 to X
until (X = 32767)	Stop repeating when X = 32767
end.	End of program

Key 13   Vector supercomputers

OVERVIEW   *Supercomputers use unconventional archi-tectures to do computations much faster than conventional computers.*

The bottlenecks in a conventional computer: Only a small part of a conventional computer is in use at any time, for two reasons:
- **No way to work on more than one memory location at the same time**. All communication between CPU and memory takes place one byte or word at a time. The rest of memory is idle. This is called the **Babbage bottleneck** and goes back to mechanical calculators made by Charles Babbage in the 19th century.
- **No way to do more than one operation at a time**. The CPU has circuits to add, multiply, compare, fetch, store, etc., but at any moment only one of these is in use; the rest of the CPU is idle. This is called the **Von Neumann bottleneck** since it stems from Von Neumann's idea of having instruction codes select particular functional units (Keys 2, 9).

Vector supercomputers: These (Cray, NEC, Fujitsu) overcome the Von Neumann bottleneck by using a single instruction code to perform the same calculations on a series of different numbers. *Example:* With a single instruction code, a Cray Y-MP can add two 64-element sequences (**vectors**) of numbers, storing the results in a third 64-element vector.
- During this 64-step process, all applicable parts of the CPU are **working simultaneously, like an assembly line**. One functional unit is adding two numbers; another is storing the result of the previous addition; another is fetching the next numbers to be added; and another is calculating the addresses of the numbers to be added after that.
- Some conventional CPUs, such as the IBM 6000, get some of the advantages of a vector machine by having **some ability use more than one functional unit at a time**. For example, such a machine can do an addition and a multiplication at the same time instead of doing one right after the other.

Key 14 Parallel computers

OVERVIEW *A parallel computer is a computer that executes more than one program or section of a program at once, thereby overcoming the Von Neumann bottleneck (Key 13).*

Multiprocessing: The simplest parallel computers have two or three CPUs running different programs while sharing i-o devices and possibly some memory. Some mainframe computers have worked this way since the 1960s, but with this setup, there is seldom any parallelism within a single program.

Parallelism: True **parallel computing** allows a single program to use more than one CPU. The programmer divides the program into sections and specifies which sections can be run simultaneously on different CPUs.

Architectures: Connections between CPUs are important in parallel computer design. It is usually not feasible to link each CPU directly to all of the others; that would require too many connections.
* One option is to link all the CPUs via a single shared **bus** (Key 6) or **ring** (compare Key 25), or through **shared memory**.
* Another is to use a **crossbar switch** to connect any CPU to any other CPU when needed.
* The **hypercube** architecture of the Intel iPSC is based on an imaginary 4-dimensional cube. It has 8 corners (CPUs) each of which is connected directly to 4 others. Any CPU can send a message to any other with at most 3 additional CPUs in between.
* **Massively parallel (connectionist)** computers use a **large number of CPUs** each of which **stores data as well as performing computations.** In effect, memory is stored in a huge array of tiny CPUs. Connectionist computers are especially good for **image processing** (Key 64) and **neural networks** (Key 73).

Power of parallel computers: Parallel computers are faster than conventional (**serial**) computers, but not, in principle, more powerful. Any parallel computer can be simulated by a serial computer.

Theme 3 OPERATING SYSTEMS

*T*he operating system of a computer is the program that controls its overall operation and enables it to run other programs. The process of starting up the operating system is called *bootstrapping* or *booting*. The operating system provides many services to the user's programs; the most important is that it maintains disk **files**, with a set of **directories** containing the names and locations of all files. Popular operating systems include UNIX, MS-DOS, VM/CMS, and graphical operating systems such as that of the Macintosh.

Key 15 "Bootstrapping"

OVERVIEW *To start up a computer, it is necessary to give the CPU some instruction codes that will cause it to read more instructions from disk, then execute them. This process is called **bootstrapping** or **booting**.*

Early computers: To start up the earliest computers, the operator had to put some instruction codes into memory by flipping switches. These instruction codes constituted a short program called a **loader**. The loader made the CPU copy further codes into memory from some i o device, such as a card reader, and then execute them.

- Typically, the first program that the CPU would load was a bigger and better loader. This, in turn, would load the user's program. So to get started, the computer had to "pull itself up by its own bootstraps," a process that came to be called **bootstrapping** or simply **booting**.

- If a program fails to terminate properly, one can **reboot** the computer (make it start afresh).

Booting a modern computer: All modern computers have some permanently recorded **read-only memory (ROM)** containing instruction codes to get them started. Thus there is no need to flip switches.

- Instead of just a loader, the computer normally loads an **operating system** into memory from disk. The operating system controls the computer when no other program is running. Part of the operating system stays in memory so that it can regain control when the user's program ends.

- The operating system can accept **commands** from the user. *Examples From IBM PC:* `dir` displays a list of files on the disk; `cls` clears the screen; `qwerty` is not a built-in command, so the operating system tries to find a program called QWERTY.EXE and run it.

- The operating system also provides **services** to users' programs. *Example:* To read data from disk, a program need not give instructions to the disk controller; it just tells the operating system, "Give me the first 52 bytes of file ABCDEF," or the like.

Key 16 Disks

OVERVIEW *For permanent data storage, most comput-ers rely on magnetic disks. These include permanently mounted* **fixed disks (hard disks)** *and removable* **dis-kettes***.*

Disks: For permanent storage of data, most computers use **magnetic media** consisting of plastic with a magnetizable coating; information is stored by magnetizing a pattern in the coating. Most computers use magnetic **disks**, either
- permanently mounted **hard disks (fixed disks)** inside the ma-chine, or
- removable **diskettes** (formerly called **floppy disks**, but the newer ones have rigid shells).

Tapes: Some computers also use **tapes**, especially for long-term backup.

Speed: Disks are many times slower than memory (RAM or ROM); tapes are slower yet. But they are cheap and permanent.

Role of the operating system: The operating system manages disk stor-age.
- Data stored on disk is arranged into **files**. Each file has a unique name and usually consists of a complete program, a word process-ing document, a graphical image, or the like.
- Each file occupies one or more **sectors** (Figure 5) on the disk. Each sector contains the same number of bytes (typically 128).
- Sectors are arranged in concentric **tracks**.
- When a new diskette is put in the computer, the user has to **format** it by running a program that creates the pattern of sectors and tracks.

Sector, cylinder, and head: A **cylinder** consists of the corresponding tracks on both sides of a diskette, or on all layers of a multi-layer fixed disk. Each side or layer has a separate **head** (magnetic read-write unit). Any location on the disk can be identified by its **sector number**, **cylinder number**, and **head number**. (The IBM PC also numbers **clusters**, which are groups of sectors.)

FIGURE 5

Each surface of a disk is organized into tracks and sectors.

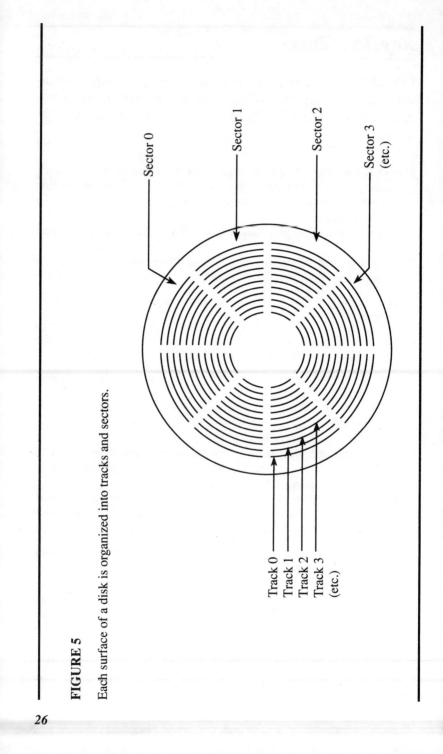

Key 17 Files

OVERVIEW *Data on disks is organized into* **files***, which are in turn grouped into* **directories***.*

Files: Programs refer to files by **file name**, not location. The sectors occupied by a file do not need to be next to each other; they can be anywhere on the disk.

Directories: In a special location on each disk, the operating system maintains a **directory** giving the names of all the files and the sectors that they occupy. Regardless of what directory a file is listed in, it can occupy space anywhere on the disk.

Reading and writing: When a program reads or writes a file, the operating system computes the appropriate locations on the disk and sends them to the disk controller.

Subdirectories: Most newer operating systems let you establish **subdirectories**, directories that reside in special files.
- The main **(root)** directory lists some files and some subdirectories containing files and/or more subdirectories. This makes it easy to keep related files together. *Example:* A file name such as \AAA\BBB\CCC\DDD means ''File DDD in directory CCC, which is in directory BBB, which is in directory AAA, which is in the root directory.''

Erase: To **erase (delete)** a file, the operating system removes the file's name from the directory and marks as empty the sectors occupied by the file. The data in those sectors, however, does not get erased until the sectors are actually needed for another file.

Unerase: Thus, if a file is erased accidentally, it is often possible to **unerase** it, provided nothing else has been written to the same area of the disk and the disk has not been formatted again.

Key 18 Operating system services

OVERVIEW *The operating system provides many services to application programs. These include creating, reading, writing, and deleting files, and access to other i-o devices such as keyboard, screen, and printer.*

Purpose: Relying on the operating system to perform i-o saves the application programmer some work. More importantly, it **insulates the program from the details of the machine** on which it is running. *Example:* The machine instructions that clear the screen are different on each of the IBM PC's many different video adapters. But a program that asks the operating system to clear the screen need not concern itself with this. The operating system will handle any video adapter correctly.

Subroutines: Programs usually obtain services through **subroutine calls**. An application program calls an operating system routine the same way that the program would call another section of its own code. The main program resumes when the subroutine finishes.

Interrupts: Some computers provide operating system services through **interrupts**. An interrupt is a special CPU instruction to interrupt a program, jump to an **interrupt service routine**, and resume the main program when the service routine finishes.
- Interrupts were originally intended to deal with external events (keys pressed, etc.). Their use as a substitute for subroutine calls has been criticized.

IBM PC: A well-known peculiarity of the IBM PC is that its operating system is divided into two parts that provide overlapping services:
- **BIOS** (Basic Input-Output System), a set of routines permanently recorded in a ROM chip
- **DOS** (Disk Operating System), which is loaded from disk

Example: To write on the screen, a program can either call DOS through interrupt 21 or call BIOS through interrupt 10, or even store data directly into video memory.

Key 19 Multitasking and virtual memory

OVERVIEW *All but the smallest computers can run more than one program at a time through **multitasking**. Most operating systems also have **virtual memory**, which is the ability to use disk space as a substitute for real memory.*

Uses for multitasking: Several people at terminals can use the same computer at once, and one person can do two kinds of work at once (e.g., editing one document while printing another).

Timesharing: Multitasking is achieved through **timesharing**. The CPU loads several programs into memory, then switches its attention back and forth between them many times per second. If one program has to wait for a keystroke, or data from disk, the CPU can work on another program rather than wasting time. *Examples:* UNIX, VAX/VMS, OS/2, and the IBM mainframe operating systems support multitasking; CP/M and MS-DOS (PC-DOS) do not.

Virtual memory: This is the use of disk space as a substitute for real memory. This is handled by the operating system; the programs use memory as if all of it were really present, and the operating system **swaps** (copies) blocks of data (**pages**) back and forth from memory to disk.

Speed: Virtual memory is slower than real memory, but the slowdown is usually not serious because most programs do not use all their data at the same time, so only a few swaps occur while running a program. However, a situation called **thrashing** sometimes occurs.
- Suppose a program is working with two data items stored at widely separate memory locations.
- Suppose further that the two items are so far apart that they get swapped out separately — each one is on disk when the other is in real memory.
- Then if the program is trying to use both data items at the same time, the operating system will be swapping almost constantly (''thrashing''). This causes a tremendous slowdown.

Key 20 UNIX

OVERVIEW *UNIX is in wide use on many different kinds of computers. It has a very versatile command language. UNIX introduced the concept of subdirectories and popularized the C programming language; a C compiler is provided with every implementation of UNIX. Innovative in many ways, it may well be the most modern operating system in wide use.*

History: UNIX was developed at Bell Laboratories in the early 1970s as a replacement for an earlier system called **Multics,** and originally distributed to educational institutions at low cost, encouraging many of the world's best programmers to work with it and contribute improvements. Several versions of UNIX are now commercial products.

Portability: Most operating systems are designed for a specific CPU, but versions of UNIX run on almost all types of computers. UNIX is easy to **port** (adapt) from one CPU to another because most of it is written, not in assembly language, but in C, a high-level language that can be compiled into efficient machine instructions. UNIX itself includes a C compiler and is largely responsible for popularizing the **C language** (Key 37).

Subdirectories: In UNIX, a disk has not only a main **(root)** directory, but also any number of additional directories **(subdirectories)** that reside in special files. A subdirectory can be listed in the main directory or in another subdirectory. File names reflect this structure. *Example:* The name (or rather **path**):
        /usr/mcovington/programs/myprog.c
implies that the root directory contains a directory called usr, which contains a directory called mcovington, which contains a directory called programs, which contains a file called myprog.c. (Strictly speaking, only myprog.c is the file name.)

Multitasking: Several people can of course use the computer simultaneously from different terminals. More importantly, each user has multiple processes; a fresh process is created for each command typed on the keyboard. Normally, UNIX waits for each command to finish before accepting the next one, but ending a command with ''&'' tells

UNIX to accept the next command immediately. *Example:* The commands

```
cc myprog.c &
ls
```

will compile myprog.c and display a list of files at the same time.

Redirection: The input and output of commands can be **redirected**. *Example:* The command sort puts the lines of a file in alphabetical order.

- If you just type sort, the sort program will try to read from the keyboard and write on the terminal, which is not too useful.
- If you type sort < aaa > bbb the sort program will read from file aaa and write its output on file bbb.
- The i-o of almost any command can be redirected in this way.

Shells: The user has a choice of several **shells** (command languages) with slightly different syntax and features **(Bourne Shell, C Shell, Korn Shell)**. All the shells allow commands to be arranged into Pascal-like programs **(shell scripts)**.

Key 21   MS-DOS and OS/2

OVERVIEW   *MS-DOS (Microsoft Disk Operating System), also known as IBM PC-DOS or simply DOS, is the operating system of the IBM PC. PC-DOS version 1 strongly resembled Digital Research CP/M, an earlier microcomputer operating system. Versions 2 and up support subdirectories and other UNIX-like features, but do not support multitasking.*

Files: Like CP/M, DOS limits file names to 11 characters of the form XXXXXXXX.XXX. The **extension** (the 3 letters after the dot) identifies the type of file; .EXE and .COM files contain machine instructions, .BAT files contain DOS commands, etc.

Wild cards: Some commands accept **wild cards** that match any file name with a specified pattern. Example: `dir v*.exe` displays a list of all files whose names begin with V and end in .EXE.

Directories: DOS **subdirectories** work like those of UNIX except that paths are written with backslashes (\ instead of /).

The 640K limit: DOS requires an Intel 8088 microprocessor or the equivalent. DOS runs on the newer Intel 80286 (PC AT), 80386, and 80486, but only when they are in 8088 compatibility mode (**real mode**). In real mode, these processors, like the 8088, are limited to 1 megabyte of memory of which the top 384K is reserved for video memory and ROM. Hence DOS is limited to 640K of general-purpose memory.

OS/2 and Windows: Unlike DOS, **OS/2** and **Microsoft Windows** (Key 23) can use the 80286, 80386, and 80486 in **protected mode**, in which the memory capacity is much larger. Protected mode is so called because it is designed for multitasking and the hardware "protects" the memory assigned to each program, preventing other programs from writing in it.

Recent developments: Originally, OS/2 and Windows could run DOS software only by dropping back to real mode and losing the ability to multitask. Later versions can use the 80386 and 80486 in **multiple virtual real mode** to emulate not just one 8088, but several, with full multitasking ability.

Key 22   OS/360, MVS, and VM/CMS

OVERVIEW   *These are IBM mainframe operating systems.*

The OS/360 family: Several versatile operating systems are descendants of **OS/360,** the operating system of the IBM 360, introduced in 1964. Later IBM mainframes such as the 370, 390, 3081, 3090, and 4341 are compatible with the 360 instruction set and use the same family of operating systems, of which the newest is called **MVS** (Multiple Virtual Storage).

Batch processing: OS/360 was originally designed for **batch processing.** Instead of sitting at terminals, users encoded their programs on punched cards and fed the stacks **(decks)** of cards into the machine. Each program to be run was called a **job.**

Timesharing: There are "add-ons" to OS/360-family operating systems that make it possible to use the computer from a terminal; these include **TSO** (Time Sharing Option) and **MUSIC** (Multi-User System for Interactive Computing).

VM/CMS: Another IBM operating system, **VM,** is designed specifically for terminal users. VM is based on a simple but powerful idea: the computer **simulates multiple copies of itself.**
  - One computer can easily simulate another. The real computer runs a program that recognizes all of the instruction codes of the simulated (virtual) computer and responds with appropriate actions. This technique is sometimes used to run IBM PC programs on Sun workstations, for instance.
  - A computer can even simulate *itself* by running a program that recognizes its *own* machine instructions. Most instructions can be passed directly to the CPU, although for purposes of the simulation, a few changes might need to be made, such as shifting memory addresses.
  - A multitasking computer can simulate *many* computers just like itself. Under VM, each user's terminal is connected to a simulation of a complete IBM 370 computer (a **virtual machine**), which runs the single-user operating system **CMS** (Conversational Monitoring System).

Key 23   Graphical operating systems

OVERVIEW   *The **Apple Macintosh operating system** is the best known, though not the first, of a new class of operating systems that use **graphical user interfaces (GUIs)**. That is, the operating system uses pictures to communicate with the user.*

How it works: On the Macintosh, programs and files are represented by **icons** (small pictures). To run a program, the user points to it with a **mouse** or other pointing device and presses (**clicks**) a button.

Windows: The screen is divided into **windows** that can overlap each other; windows can be moved around with the mouse, and a window that is hidden can be brought back into view with its contents intact.

Menus: There are also plenty of **menus** (lists of choices) that can be brought into view, and on which the user can make choices by using just the mouse without typing on the keyboard.

User interface: To a remarkable extent, all Macintosh programs look alike, so anyone who knows how to use one program can quickly learn to use others.
- This similarity is due to the fact that the operating system, rather than the application program, handles nearly all communication with the user.
- Ordinary operating systems just transmit characters on the screen, and if there are to be menus, the application program must create them character by character.
- Graphical operating systems, however, know how to display menus, prompt the user to choose a file, and even edit text; application programs can do all these things through operating system services.

Earlier graphical user interfaces: Xerox Star word processor, Xerox 1100 Lisp machine, and Lisp machines developed at MIT (Key 67).

Other graphical operating systems on the market today: OS/2 version 1.1 and higher (Key 21), **Microsoft Windows**, and several graphical user interfaces for UNIX, including **SunView** and **Xwindows**. Most of these multitask by putting a separate process in each window.

Relation to object-oriented programming: Because the services provided by a graphical operating system are so elaborate, it can be hard to write a program to use them effectively. Since the earliest Lisp machines, programmers have used **object-oriented** techniques (Key 33) to simplify this task.

- Instead of just calling procedures, the application program "sends messages" to **objects** such as windows and menus, which respond with appropriate actions.
- Most of these "messages" originate as **events** such as keystrokes, mouse movements, and the like.
- In effect, there is no "main program" and the user, rather than the program, calls procedures.

Theme 4 DATA COMMUNICATION

*D*ata communication is the exchange of information among computers. It is becoming an increasingly important area of computer technology. The main kinds of data communication are parallel and serial cables between parts of a computer system, local area networking, and wide area networking.

Key 24 Parallel and serial communication

OVERVIEW *A cable can carry data in either of two forms, **parallel** or **serial**. Parallel communication is faster and is usually used with printers; serial communication is used to connect computers to terminals.*

Parallel: The 8 bits of each character travel simultaneously on 8 wires. This is fast (often used with printers), but the cable must be fairly short.

Serial: The 8 bits of a character travel one after another on a single wire. This is slow but allows a long cable (no crosstalk between wires).

Terminals: Almost always use serial communication. A terminal consists of a screen (cathode-ray tube, **CRT**) and a keyboard. A microcomputer running **terminal emulation software** can be used as a terminal.

RS-232 serial communication: Most serial communication systems follow the **EIA-232 (RS-232)** standard, which specifies the signal voltages but leaves it up to the user to choose the **baud rate**, the number of bits per character (7 or 8), and the **parity**.

Baud rate: Is the maximum number of signals that can be sent per second. Since RS-232 has only two kinds of signals, 0 and 1, the baud rate for RS-232 signals is equal to the number of bits per second (**bps**). Allowing for the **start bit** and **stop bit** between characters, the bps rate is 10 times the number of characters transmitted per second (2400 baud = 240 cps).

Parity: Refers to an extra bit that is sometimes added so that the total number of 1's in each character is always even (or always odd). This makes it possible to detect characters garbled in transmission.

Modems: Data can be transmitted over telephone lines using a **modem** (modulator-demodulator), which converts RS-232 serial signals into sounds that the telephone can transmit. **Hayes compatible** modems can dial their own phone calls.

ISDN: Modems will eventually be obsolete because telephone companies will provide digital lines directly to the customer. This is known as Integrated Services Digital Network (**ISDN**).

Key 25   Local area networking

OVERVIEW   *A **local area network (LAN)** links computers in the same building so that they can share files or printers. One computer, the **server**, can provide disk space for several others. The **topology** of a LAN is the shape in which the machines are connected together—ring, star (with one at the center), or bus (all in parallel).*

Ethernet: LANs require fast communications, so most LANs use some form of **Ethernet**, a communication technology developed by Xerox that uses radio-frequency signals inside a coaxial cable. (Radio waves were once thought to be vibrations of a substance called ''ether'' or ''aether,'' hence the name.)

- On an Ethernet, all the computers share the same cable and each can receive signals from any other. Data is organized into **packets** each of which has a **header** stating which computer it is addressed to.

- If two computers transmit at the same time (a ''collision''), they retry again after random lengths of time. This is called **CSMA/CD** (carrier sense, multiple access, collision detection).

Token-ring: In a **token-ring** network, a special message, the **token**, is passed around the ring, and only the computer that has the token is allowed to transmit. One advantage of a token ring is that there is no limit on the total cable length, as long as the individual computers are close enough together, because each computer retransmits every message to the next computer.

TCP/IP: To share files and printers, the operating system must support networking. UNIX systems normally adhere to a U.S. Department of Defense standard called **TCP/IP** (Transmission Control Protocol/ Internet Protocol).

- ftp command: transfer files from one computer to another
- telnet command: use any computer as terminal on any other

NFS: The Sun Microsystems **Network File System (NFS)** is an emerging standard that lets each networked UNIX machine read and write files and even execute programs on the others.

Key 26 Wide area networking

OVERVIEW *A **wide-area network (WAN)** connects computers that are many miles apart. WANs are used mainly to transmit **electronic mail (email)**. Each computer on the network is called a **node** and is frequently called on to pass along messages to other machines.*

Usenet: One of the oldest WANs is **Usenet** (sometimes called **UUCP**), established by an organization of UNIX users. Usenet uses fast cable connections when they exist, but when they do not, it passes messages along by using modems to make phone calls automatically. Isolated computer users can join Usenet with no special equipment other than a modem.

BITNET and Internet: BITNET was originally established to link universities in the Northeast. **Internet** (formerly **ARPANET**) was originally set up by the Defense Advanced Research Projects Agency (ARPA). These nets and Usenet are now linked; mail is sent in Internet format. BITNET and Internet rely on high-speed cable links.

KEY EXAMPLE

An Internet address

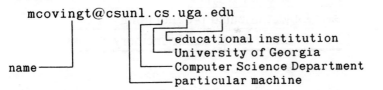

```
mcovingt@csun1.cs.uga.edu
```
- educational institution
- University of Georgia
- Computer Science Department
- particular machine
- name

To pass along a message to this address, a computer along the way need not know where `csun1` or even `cs` is, as long as it can find `uga.edu`.

Forwarding: In addresses, "`%`" stands for "`@`" when messages are to be forwarded. *Example:* `mcovingt%uga.bitnet@cunyvm.cuny.edu` means "Send this message to the computer called `cunyvm.cuny.edu`, which will know how to send it on to `mcovingt@uga.bitnet`."

Theme 5 PROGRAMMING LANGUAGE DESIGN

*C*omputer programs are usually written in programming languages rather than machine code. Each programming language is designed to describe computations precisely while being easy for humans to use. This Theme surveys general issues in programming language design; Theme 6 covers particular languages.

Key 27   Syntax and semantics

OVERVIEW   *The syntax of a language determines what statements are possible, and how they are written; the semantics determines what these statements make the computer do.*

The art of language design: Beginning programmers often think that programming languages must, for technical reasons, be exactly as they are. This is not true. Programming languages are designed by human beings, and programmers should be able to critique the design of a language.

Syntactic design issues: These refer to the way statements are written.
- Does each statement have to begin on a new line? (Yes in Fortran and early BASIC; no in Pascal and C.)
- Are there **reserved words** which the user cannot redefine for other purposes? If so, is the set of reserved words small and restricted, or will it grow in future versions of the language? (If more reserved words are added, user-defined names that are legal today may be illegal tomorrow; this has happened in Microsoft BASIC.)
- Does the user have to declare variable names before using them? (Yes in Pascal and C, no in BASIC. Because of this, a BASIC compiler cannot detect a misspelled variable name; it just treats it as another variable.)

Semantic design issues: These refer to what the statements make the computer do. The designer must decide what **elementary types** of data the language will handle—numbers, character strings, files, etc.—and what **elementary operations** will be available.
- Turbo Pascal, for instance, has elementary operations on strings of characters; ISO Standard Pascal does not.
- Fortran supports arithmetic on complex numbers $(x + y\sqrt{-1})$; Pascal and C do not. In Pascal and C, complex-number arithmetic has to be defined by the programmer in terms of simpler operations.
- The language must express the elementary operations in a readable way. A selling point of Fortran in 1958 was that it allowed mathematicians to write A=B+C instead of LOAD B, ADD C, STORE A. This made arithmetic not only easier, but also less error-prone.

Key 28 Data types and operations

OVERVIEW *This Key surveys the types of data available in several programming languages and the operations that can be performed on them.*

KEY EXAMPLE

A Pascal program

```
program a;
var x,y,z: integer;
begin
  read(x,y);
  z := x+y;
  write(z)
end.
```

Here x, y, and z are **variables** that hold values of type **integer** (positive and negative whole numbers).

The **statements** read(x,y), z := x+y, and write(z) tell the computer to read two numbers into x and y, store the sum of x and y into z, and then write out the contents of z.

Integers: Inside the computer, x, y, and z are binary, not decimal (see Key 53), and there are limits on their size. On a 16-bit CPU, for example, integers range from $-32,768$ to $32,767$. Some languages also provide **unsigned integers** that range from 0 to 65,535 (the largest number that will fit in 16 bits).

Floating-point numbers: Almost all programming languages also allow computations on **floating-point numbers** (numbers with a fractional part). "Floating-point" means that the decimal point can come anywhere; 1.2345, 12.345, and 123.45 are all 5-digit floating-point numbers.

Mantissa and exponent: Floating-point numbers are stored as a **mantissa** and **exponent**. With decimal numbers, this is what we call **scientific notation**: 0.00123 would be described as 1.23×10^{-3} (mantissa 1.23, exponent -3). On the computer, this is written $1.23E-3$ (a notation called **E format**). Internally, however, the mantissa and exponent are binary.

Character data: Most languages also do computations on **character strings**. The most common operations are to **concatenate** strings (e.g., "George" + "Washington" = "George Washington") and to compare them with respect to alphabetical order ("George" < "Georgia").

SNOBOL: The programming language SNOBOL is designed specifically for character string processing. It has built-in operations to match patterns in strings.

Symbolic expressions: Lisp and Prolog support computations on **symbolic expressions**. A symbolic expression is a formula written in the same notation as the program itself. **Example:** (A B (C D)) is a **list** in Lisp (with another list inside it), and family(father(michael),daughter(sharon)) is a **structure** in Prolog.

- These are not character strings; the computer recognizes their internal structure and represents them in an efficient way using pointers (Key 34).
- Symbolic expressions are a convenient way to represent very complex information. They are widely used in artificial intelligence (Keys 65–73).

Key 29   Subprograms and modularity

OVERVIEW   *To prevent errors, it is important to divide a program cleanly into sections. This is called **modularity**. One way to make a program modular is to divide it into **subprograms**, of which there are two kinds, **procedures** and **functions**.*

Procedures: Here is a Pascal procedure which, given a number *n*, prints *n* blank lines:

```
procedure skiplines(n:integer);
var i: integer;
begin
 for i:=1 to n do writeln
end;
```

- This procedure has one **argument (parameter)**, an integer called n, and one **local variable**, called i, which exists only within the procedure.
- The main program calls a procedure by executing a statement such as skiplines(10) (in Pascal) or CALL SKIPLINES(10) (in Fortran).
- This gives the value 10 to the parameter n and starts executing skiplines. When the procedure finishes, the main program resumes.
- In effect, defining this procedure adds a new statement, skiplines, to the Pascal language.

Functions: Functions are like procedures except that a function **returns a value**. Function calls are not statements; they are used in expressions. **Example:** z := 2+sqrt(y) finds the square root of y using the function sqrt, then adds 2 and stores the result in z.

- Crucially, sqrt(y) has a value (the square root of y); skiplines(y) does not have a value, although it does perform an action.

Lisp and C: Lisp and C blur the distinction between procedures and functions. In these languages, all procedures return values, but the value can be discarded. In C, for instance, sqrt(z) is a perfectly legal (but pointless) statement that computes the square root of z and then does nothing with it. By contrast, the statement x = sqrt(z) finds the value of sqrt(z) and stores it in the variable x.

Key 30 Structured programming

OVERVIEW *Structured programming is a technique for writing programs efficiently and avoiding errors. It generally includes neat, readable layout, modularity (Key 29), carefully planned data structures (Keys 31–32), and avoidance of GO TO statements.*

KEY EXAMPLES

Both in BASIC:

Unstructured program	*Structured program*
10 LET X=1	10 LET X=1
20 IF X>1000 GO TO 60	20 WHILE X<=1000
30 PRINT X	30 PRINT X
40 LET X=X+X	40 LET X=X+X
50 GO TO 20	50 WEND

"GO TO statement considered harmful"(—Dijkstra): In older computer languages, a program was a list of things for the computer to do, and decisions were made by jumping from place to place in the list. See the left-hand example above. In 1968, E. W. Dijkstra pointed out that **GO TO statements are error-prone** because the programmer doesn't see the path of execution leading to a particular statement.

GO-TO-less programming: Dijkstra and colleagues advocated **GO-TO-less programming**, replacing all GO TO statements with alternatives like **block-structured IFs, repeat loops,** and **while loops**.

- A **while loop** keeps repeating something as long as a condition is true. For example, see the right-hand example above.
- A **repeat loop** is like a while loop, but the condition is tested at the end instead of the beginning.
- A **block-structured IF** contains blocks (groups) of statements, such as:

```
if x>y then
  begin
    y := y+1; x := x-1
  end
else
  begin
    x := x+1; y := y-1
  end;
```

Key 31 Data structures

OVERVIEW *Data structures are ways of grouping information together.*

Arrays: Almost all programming languages have a data structure called an **array**. The **elements** of an array are **all the same type** and are identified by a number called the **subscript**.

KEY EXAMPLE

The Pascal declaration
```
var x: array[1..100] of integer;
```
creates 100 integer variables known as x[1], x[2], ... x[100].

Subscript: Crucially, the **subscript** (the identifying number) can be computed while the program is running and used as a way of **deciding which element to process**.

KEY EXAMPLE

The loop
```
for i:=1 to 100 do writeln(x[i]);
```
will print out all the elements of x, one by one. Nothing like this would be possible if there were simply 100 variables with 100 different names.

Records: Pascal and C also have **records** (in C called **structs**), in which the elements (called **fields**) are of **different types** and are identified by **name**.

KEY EXAMPLE

Suppose a student in a class has a name, 2 homework grades, and 1 exam grade. This information could be collected together in a record variable such as:

```
var x: record
          name: string;
          hwk1,
          hwk2,
          exam: integer
        end;
```

The fields are referred to as x.name, x.hwk1, x.hwk2, and x.exam.

Arrays of records: There can also be **arrays of records** and **records of arrays**. A whole class of students might be represented by an array of 40 records like the one above. If there were 10 homework grades per student, instead of 2, it would be useful to treat them as an array within the record. This would be declared as:

```
var x: array[1..40] of
        record
          name: string;
          hwk: array[1..10] of integer;
          exam: integer
        end;
```

This is an array of records, and each record has another array as one of its fields. In this structure, the 4th homework grade of the 18th student would be stored in the element called x[18].hwk[4].

Key 32   User-defined types

OVERVIEW   *The Pascal language introduced the important idea that each kind of record or array is a **new data type** (alongside the built-in types* real, integer, *etc.) and that the user ought to be able to give names to these **user-defined types**.*

Naming kinds of records and arrays: Let's give names to each kind of record or array in the previous example:

```
type homeworkgrades =
  array [1..10] of integer;
type studentgrades =
  record
   name: string;
   hwk: homeworkgrades;
   exam: integer
  end;
type classgrades =
  array [1..40] of studentgrades;
var x: classgrades;
```

The elements of x are still referred to the same way as before, but the organization is clearer, and the types homeworkgrades, studentgrades, and classgrades can be used as needed elsewhere in the program.

Enumerated types: Pascal also allows **enumerated types,** in which the values themselves are invented by the user. *Example:*
type kindofstudent = (undergrad, graduate, postdoc);
- This creates a type whose possible values are undergrad, graduate, and postdoc, with a unique arbitrary bit pattern for each.
- Statements such as x := undergrad or if y = postdoc then . . . are possible, provided x and y are of type kindofstudent.

Subranges: Pascal also provides **subranges,** user-defined types that span limited ranges of some other type (usually integers). *Example:* var k: 1..100 lets k only have values in the range 1 to 100; trying to assign it any other value causes a runtime error.

Key 33 Object-oriented programming

OVERVIEW *An **object type** or **class** is a user-defined type that has procedures associated with it. **Objects** (values) belonging to the type are called **instances** of it. In **object-oriented programming (OOP)**, the whole program is organized in terms of object types.*

Object types: Programmers have always written procedures to process their user-defined types. What's new about object-oriented programming is that the **procedures and functions are explicitly associated with the types**, through declarations such as this (in Turbo Pascal 5.5):

```
type studentgrades =
   object
    name: string;
    hwk: homeworkgrades;
    exam: integer;
    procedure average { defined elsewhere }
   end;
```

- If x is a variable of type studentgrades, then the average procedure associated with it is called by the statement x.average (not average(x) as you might expect, even though x does get passed to the procedure).
- Early object-oriented programming systems referred to this as "sending the message average to object x" and even used statements such as (send x :average). But **"message-sending" is not the main idea of object-oriented programming**; it's just a metaphor for describing it.

Polymorphism: The programmer can define procedures with the same names for different types **(polymorphism)**. The computer keeps track of which procedures belong to which types. As a result, **similar operations on different types can be given the same name**.

Subtypes: One object type can be defined as a **subtype** of another, so that it **inherits** the structure and procedures of the type on which it is based, except for any that are explicitly overridden.

Key 34 Pointers and dynamic memory

OVERVIEW   *Pascal and C support **pointers**. A pointer is a variable containing the memory address of another variable.*

Main uses for pointers:
- To **decide at run time which variable to use**. In this sense pointers are like array subscripts, but more general, because they can point to anything. By using pointers, a record can contain the address of another record, or even itself (Key 45).
- To refer to **dynamically created variables**.

Dynamically created variables: The statements new (in Pascal) and malloc (in C) create new variables while a program is running. Such variables have no names because they did not exist when the program was written; they have to be referred to via pointers.

Uses: Dynamically allocated variables are used whenever a program does not know in advance how much memory it will need.

KEY EXAMPLE

A Pascal program that does several things with pointers:

```
program pointerexample;
var
 i,j: integer;
 p,q: ^integer;     { pointers to integer }
begin
 i := 123;
 p := addr(i);      { p contains address of i }
 q := p;            { now q also contains address of i }
 writeln(q^);       { write out what q points to,
                      namely 123 }
 q^ := q^+1;        { equivalent to i:=i+1 }
 writeln(p^);       { p also points to i, so it writes
                      124 }
 new(q);            { create new integer and make q
                      point to it }
 q^ := p^+1;        { store 124+1 in the new variable}
 new(p);            { create new integer and make p
                      point to it }
 p^ := 0;           { store 0 in this new variable }
 writeln(p^,q^);    { writes 0 and 125 }
 new(p);            { create yet another variable }
{ The variable that p previously pointed to is
  irretrievably lost, because nothing now points
  to it and it has no name. }
end.
```

Theme 6 SPECIFIC PROGRAMMING LANGUAGES

*T*his Theme briefly surveys several widely used programming languages. Pascal, Modula-2, and Ada are closely related languages designed for structured programming; C is designed for efficient and concise code; C++ is an object-oriented extension of C; and BASIC, Fortran, and COBOL date from before the structured programming era.

Key 35 Pascal

OVERVIEW *The programming language **Pascal** was developed in order to promote structured programming and to show that a simple language could be powerful enough for serious work. Pascal is very widely used on microcomputers and is a good language for describing algorithms.*

Origin: Pascal was developed by Niklaus Wirth around 1971. It is named for Blaise Pascal, who built a mechanical computer around 1642. Wirth developed Pascal as a simpler alternative to **Algol**, which had been designed by an international committee.

Versions:
- **ISO standard Pascal** (derived from Wirth's work): no variable-length character strings, no way to compile procedures separately from the main program, hence no way to build a procedure library.
- **UCSD Pascal** (U. of California, 1970s) allowed programmers to define **units** (groups of procedures) and compile them separately.
- **Turbo Pascal** (implemented by Anders Hejlsberg in Denmark, marketed by Borland International) has units, variable-length strings, and many other valuable extensions. Available on IBM PC and Macintosh only.

KEY EXAMPLE

A Pascal program

```
program pascaldemo(output);
var i: integer;
begin
 x := 1;
 while x<1000 do
  begin
   writeln(x); x := x + x
  end
end.
```

The keywords `begin` and `end` enclose **blocks** of statements. A begin-end block can go anywhere a single statement can go.
Many features of Pascal are discussed in Keys 27–34.

Key 36   Modula-2 and Ada

OVERVIEW *Modula and its successor Modula-2 were developed by Niklaus Wirth in the early 1980s as a successor to Pascal, which Wirth had designed a decade earlier. Ada is a full-featured Pascal-like language developed for the U.S. Department of Defense.*

Modula-2: Modula-2 is similar to Pascal but solves the problem of how to compile subprograms separately from the main program. Programs are divided into **modules** each of which can **export** names to, and **import** names from, other modules. Modules can be compiled separately.

KEY EXAMPLE

A Modula-2 program

```
MODULE Modula2demo;
FROM InOut IMPORT WriteInt, WriteLn;
VAR x: INTEGER;
BEGIN
 x := 1;
 WHILE x<1000 DO
  x := x+x; WriteInt(i,5); WriteLn
 END
END Modula2demo.
```

Differences from Pascal: One big difference is that a subprogram can determine the size of an array at run time; this is the key to implementing variable-length strings.
   - In Modula-2, Read, Write, WriteInt, etc., are ordinary procedures with fixed numbers and types of arguments; this impairs conciseness but allows users to write their own substitutes for them.
   - Modula-2 includes a mechanism to handle **concurrent processes**.

Ada: A full-featured, powerful Pascal-like language developed for the U.S. Department of Defense, Ada is named for Augusta Ada Byron (1815-1852), the world's first programmer, who worked with a mechanical computer built by Charles Babbage.

Purpose: Ada is specifically designed for **embedded systems** (computers that control equipment) as well as general-purpose computing.

Use: The name Ada is a registered trademark and can only legally be used for compilers that have passed a **validation suite** of official test programs. This, combined with the language's complexity, has made the use of Ada expensive and somewhat uncommon.

Form: In Ada, **semicolons** come *after* statements (as in C) rather than *between* them as in Pascal and Modula-2. Every Ada statement ends with a semicolon regardless of what follows it.

KEY EXAMPLE

An Ada program

```
WITH Basic_IO;
USE Basic_IO;
PROCEDURE Ada_Demo IS
  x. Integer := 1;
BEGIN
  WHILE x < 1000 LOOP
  x := x + x; Put(x); NewLine;
  END LOOP;
END AdaDemo;
```

Key 37   C and C++

OVERVIEW   *C was designed at Bell Laboratories and a C compiler is included in every copy of the operating system UNIX (Key 20). C is designed so that the compiler can translate it into very efficient machine code. C++ is an object-oriented extension of C.*

Origin of C: The programming language **C** was designed by Dennis Ritchie at Bell Laboratories around 1972 and was used to write much of the operating system **UNIX** (Key 20). C replaced an earlier language called B. More recently, C has become very popular for programming all types of small computers.

KEY EXAMPLE

A C program

```
#include <stdio.h>
main( )
{
  int x = 1;
  while (x<1000)
   { x += x; printf( "%d\n",x); }
  return(0);
}
```

Here #include <stdio.h> tells the compiler to read the **header file** STDIO.H, which tells it how to call the standard i-o library.

Semicolons come after statements (as in Ada), not between them as in Pascal. In C, every statement ends with a semicolon regardless of what comes after it.

The statement x += x means the same thing as x = x + x. Even more concisely, x++ would mean x = x + 1.

Advantages of C:

- C programs tend to be efficient because **operations that are easy for the CPU are easy to express in C**, and those that are hard for the CPU are hard in C. *Example:* Comparison of numbers uses the operator > because the CPU can compare numbers directly, but comparison of strings requires a procedure call in C because that is how the CPU does it.

- Many **operating system services** (Key 18) are available — even the ability to load and run another program. Traditionally, when C is implemented on non-UNIX systems, the operating system calls are made as much like UNIX as possible. Thus **the power of UNIX carries over**, in C, to other operating systems.

C++: Developed in the mid-1980s by Bjarne Stroustrup (also of Bell Labs), C++ extends C by adding **object-oriented programming** (Key 33). The goal of C++ is to make all data types equally easy for the programmer to handle, regardless of whether the tasks are equally easy for the CPU. In this respect C++ is quite different from C.

- In C++, user-defined types (**classes**) can **inherit** the attributes of other object classes.

- C++ even allows the programmer to define what **operators** such as +, −, *, etc., do to objects other than numbers. Thus + could denote concatenation of strings or vector addition of vectors.

Key 38 BASIC

OVERVIEW *BASIC (Beginner's All-Purpose Symbolic Instruction Code) was the first language designed for interactive computing. It was originally elegant and simple in design, but later microcomputer versions have become very complicated.*

Origin: The programming language **BASIC** (Beginner's All-Purpose Symbolic Instruction Code) was invented in 1964 by John Kemeny and Thomas Kurtz.

Goals: It was designed for **interactive computing** (computing at a terminal, rather than batch processing; see Key 22). One design goal for BASIC was that a person knowing even a small part of the language should be able to get useful results.

Programs: Programs are short and variable names need not be declared in advance. Each statement begins with a line number, important because terminals in 1964 were **teletype machines**, with no way to move the cursor to make corrections. The programmer could only correct a line by retyping it. The computer used the line numbers to keep the lines in order.

Subsequent development: BASIC is the most complicated programming language in wide use today.
- At first BASIC was used mainly to do mathematical calculations. It included MAT (matrix) statements to do matrix arithmetic.
- BASIC lost its elegant simplicity in the 1970s when it became popular on microcomputers. The MAT statements were dropped but hundreds of new kinds of statements were added in an unplanned way. **Microsoft BASIC** on the IBM PC has about 300 **reserved words** (Key 27), and it's a safe bet nobody remembers the entire list.

KEY EXAMPLE

A BASIC program

```
10 INPUT X
20 LET Y = SQR(X)
30 PRINT "THE SQUARE ROOT OF", X, "IS", Y
40 END
```

Key 39 Fortran

OVERVIEW *Fortran (Formula translation), introduced by IBM in 1958, was the first programming language that allowed programmers to express mathematical expressions as formulas, for example writing A=B+C instead of* LOAD B, ADD C, STORE A. *Fortran introduced important concepts such as **arrays (Key 31) and subroutines (Key 29).***

The Fortran language: Fortran has always been well standardized, making this a good language in which to write **portable** programs (programs easily converted from one computer to another).

Variations: Fortran II was used briefly in the early 1960s, then replaced by **Fortran IV** and, later, **Fortran 77** (1977). Of these, Fortran IV remains the most widely recognized standard.

Layout: Fortran was designed for punched cards. Any line beginning with C is a comment. Statement labels appear in columns 2-5 and statements begin in column 7.

FORMAT statements: The statement PRINT 100, I in the sample program refers to a **format** statement labeled 100. This format statement could be placed anywhere in the program. It specifies how to print a number: one blank (1X) followed by a 6-digit integer (I6).

Carriage control: The first character of each line of output is not printed, but instead is used for **carriage control** (printer control): blank to begin a new line, '0' to skip an extra line, '1' to begin a new page, or '+' to overprint on the same line.

KEY EXAMPLE

A Fortran IV program

```
C SAMPLE OF FORTRAN IV - M. COVINGTON 1990
      INTEGER I
      I = 1
   1  PRINT 100, I
 100  FORMAT(1X,I6)
      I = I+I
      IF (I.LE.1000) GO TO 1
      STOP
      END
```

Key 40 COBOL

OVERVIEW *COBOL (Common Business-Oriented Language) is unique because it looks like English. COBOL was developed in the early 1960s and is still used in business data processing. Programs are very easy to read, but complex algorithms are hard to express.*

Important features of COBOL:

- COBOL introduced the **record** data structure (Key 31) and gave programmers detailed control over the storage of data in memory.
- In COBOL, numbers are often stored as character strings of decimal digits rather than as binary numbers.
- Decimal arithmetic avoids the **rounding errors** that result from conversion to binary (see Key 53).

A COBOL program

```
IDENTIFICATION DIVISION.

PROGRAM-ID. COBOL-DEMO.
AUTHOR.    M. A. COVINGTON.

ENVIRONMENT DIVISION.

CONFIGURATION SECTION.
SOURCE-COMPUTER. IBM-PC.
OBJECT-COMPUTER. IBM-PC.

DATA DIVISION.

WORKING-STORAGE SECTION.
77  SUM PICTURE IS S999999, USAGE IS COMPUTATIONAL.
77  X   PICTURE IS S999999, USAGE IS COMPUTATIONAL.

PROCEDURE DIVISION.

START-UP.
   MOVE 0 TO SUM.
GET-A-NUMBER.
   DISPLAY "TYPE A NUMBER: " UPON CONSOLE.
   ACCEPT X FROM CONSOLE.
   IF X IS EQUAL TO 0 GO TO FINISH.
   ADD X TO SUM.
   GO TO GET-A-NUMBER.
FINISH.
   DISPLAY SUM UPON CONSOLE.
   STOP RUN.
```

Theme 7 ALGORITHMS

*A*n algorithm is an exact procedure for doing a computation. This Theme surveys some important algorithms and some ways of organizing data for efficient processing.

Key 41   Searching

OVERVIEW *A common problem is to find a particular element (called the* **target***) in an array. Finding a particular name in a phone book is an instance of this problem. There are three main techniques:* **sequential search***,* **binary search***, and* **hashing***.*

Sequential search: The simplest approach: look at each element, starting with the first, then the second, and so on, until the desired element is found. This takes time proportional to the number of elements in the array.

Binary search (interval-halving search): Possible only if the elements are stored in alphabetical or numeric order.
- Start by comparing the target to the element in the exact middle of the array. This will tell you whether it should be in the first half or the second half. Then take whichever half of the array the target falls into, and compare the target to the middle element of that.
- Keep doing this with smaller and smaller sections of the array until you find the target or end up with a section with 0 elements, which will prove that the target is not in the array.
- Binary search takes time proportional to $\log_2 n$, where n is the number of elements in the array. For example, any element in a million-element array can be found in fewer than 21 steps.
- An alternative to an array is a **binary tree** (Key 45), which is a data structure with the binary search built into it.

Hashing: A **hash function** is an arbitrary function which, given any value, picks out an array location where that value should be stored. This can be any function at all, as long as it always gives the same location for the same value.
- When the array is built, each element is stored where the hash function says it should be stored, or in the next available location if that location is already taken.
- To find an element, simply apply the hash function to it, and search forward from the location that the hash function specifies.

Key 42   Sorting

OVERVIEW   *Another common problem is to sort the elements of an array (arrange them into numeric or alphabetical order).*

Desired characteristics: A good sorting algorithm should do the sorting **in place** (without making another copy of the array) and should be **stable** (so that if two elements are alike, their relative order is not disturbed). Stability is important when the same array is sorted more than once on different fields, e.g., by first and then by last name.

KEY EXAMPLE

A selection sort

Suppose you are sorting an array A with elements numbered from 1 to n. To start, find the smallest element in A[1]...A[n] and swap it with A[1]. Then find the smallest element in A[2]...A[n] and swap it with A[2], and so on until you reach the end of the list. In Pascal:

```
for i:=1 to n−1 do
  begin
    smallest :=i;
    for j:=i+1 to n do
      if A[j] < A[smallest] then smallest:=j;
    swap(A[smallest],A[i])
  end;
```

The complete sort takes about n swaps and about $n^2/2$ comparisons.

Insertion sort: Also takes time proportional to n^2 except that it is much faster if only a few elements are out of place (e.g., adding elements to a sorted array). Suppose you're alphabetizing the letters in the string ACDBFE.
- Start at the beginning and search for a letter that is out of sequence. The first such letter is B.
- Shift it leftward past all the letters that should come after it—that is, make it jump over C and D. Now you have ABCDFE.
- Starting where you put B down, again search for the first letter that is out of sequence. This time you'll get E. Now shift E leftward past F, giving ABCDEF. No more letters are out of sequence, so now you're done.

Key 43 Quicksort

OVERVIEW *The **Quicksort** algorithm, invented by C. A. R. Hoare, takes time proportional to $n \log_2 n$ (much less than n^2) to sort a random array. It is a **recursive** algorithm—that is, it solves a problem by dividing it into smaller problems of the same kind.*

How Quicksort works: The key idea is to **partition** the array so that:
- one element (the **pivot**) gets into its final position;
- all elements that should precede the pivot get put before it;
- all elements that should follow the pivot get put after it.

Then sort the two **sub-arrays** (portions of the original array) before and after the pivot, and you're done. *Example:* To put the letters QWERTYZXCVBNM into alphabetical order, you might choose Q as the pivot, then partition the array into ECBNM + Q + RTYZXV, then sort ECBNM and RTYZXV.

Recursion (Key 44): In order to do a Quicksort on an array, you have to do two smaller Quicksorts on the sub-arrays. That's **recursion**. The process does not continue endlessly because you'll eventually get sub-arrays with only 0 or 1 elements, and you don't have to sort them.

Partitioning in place (without making copies of the array): First, choose the pivot arbitrarily. (In the example, we use the first element as the pivot. This is not such a good idea if the array is already nearly sorted; it would be better to pick a random element.) Then search the remainder of the array from both ends:
- Starting at the beginning, look for the first element that should follow the pivot.
- Meanwhile, starting at the end, look for the first element that should precede the pivot.
- When you find two such elements, swap them, then continue the search.
- Keep going until the two searches bump into each other. Divide the array in two at that place.
- Finally, swap the pivot with the first element of the second sub-array.

Disadvantages: Unlike insertion sort and selection sort, Quicksort is not **stable** (Key 42). Nor is it efficient for arrays that are already almost sorted (it has no way of realizing that, in such a case, very few elements need to be moved).

KEY EXAMPLE

Quicksort in Pascal

```
{ Quicksort for array a[1..n] }
procedure swap(var x,y: char);
var
 t: ...same type as elements of a...;
begin
 t:=x; x:=y; y:=t
end;


procedure partition(first,last:integer;
                                var p:integer);
{ Partitions a[first]...a[last] into two }
{ sub-arrays using a[first] as pivot. }
{ p is position where pivot ends up. }
var
 i, j: integer;
 pivot: ...same type as elements of a...;
begin
 pivot := a[first];
 i:=first;
 j:=last+1;
 repeat
  repeat i:=i+1 until (a[i]>=pivot) or (i=last);
  repeat j:=j-1 until (a[j]<=pivot) or (j=first);
  if i<j then swap(a[i],a[j])
 until j<=i;
 swap(a[j],a[first]);
 p := j
end;


procedure quicksort(first,last:integer);
 { Sorts the sub-array from a[first] to a[last] }
var p: integer;
begin
 if first >= last then exit;
 partition(first,last,p);
 quicksort(first,p-1);
 quicksort(p+1,last)
end;
```

Key 44 Recursion

OVERVIEW *Recursion is what happens when a proce-dure calls itself. Recursion is a way to solve problems by decomposing them into smaller problems of the same kind.*

Where recursion is used: Some problems for which recursion is useful include:
- **Quicksort** (Key 43);
- **searching binary trees** (Key 45);
- **translating arithmetic expressions into machine code** (because an expression such as (2+3) + (4+5) contains smaller expressions, 2+3 and 4+5, within it).
- There are also many others. The programming languages Lisp and Prolog use recursion to describe all kinds of repetitive processes.

How to understand recursion: If you think of a program as a list of things for the machine to do, you will have a hard time understanding recursion. After all, it makes no sense to re-start a list when you are already in the middle of it. But if you think in terms of **defining procedures**, recursion is easy to understand.
- It makes perfect sense, in the middle of a procedure, to perform the same procedure on a smaller problem.
- For example, in the process of cleaning your house, you clean the kitchen, which is part of the house.

How recursion is implemented: Pascal and C support recursion; that is, they allow procedures and functions to call themselves. (BASIC and Fortran usually do not.)
- When a procedure calls itself, the computer creates a **whole new copy of the procedure**, or more precisely a **new set of parameters and local variables**; this keeps the called procedure from interfering with the caller, even if they are the same procedure.

Recursive program logic: Any repetitive procedure can be expressed recursively.

KEY EXAMPLE

Here is a recursive procedure that just prints the numbers 1 to 10:

```
procedure printnumbers(n:integer);
begin
 writeln(n);
 if n<10 then printnumbers(n+1)
end;
```

This is started by calling `printnumbers(1)`.

Of course recursion is no particular help in this algorithm; it would be more efficient to use a `for` loop. Recursion is normally used only when it makes the algorithm easier to express.

Alternatives: Conversely, **any recursive algorithm can be expressed without recursion**, although it is sometimes very cumbersome to do so.

Termination: Every recursive procedure must have a situation in which it does *not* call itself, and must work toward that situation; otherwise the recursion is endless.

Key 45 Lists and trees

OVERVIEW *A **linked list** is a set of data items each of which includes the location of the next item in the list. A **tree** is similar, but each element can include the locations of two or more additional elements.*

Linked lists: Linked lists are useful because elements can be added, removed, or re-ordered by changing just the pointers, without actually moving the elements (Figure 6 A, B). By contrast, addding or removing an element of an array requires shifting all the adjacent elements to make room or fill the gap.

Building lists: Lists are usually built from **dynamically allocated memory** with **pointers** (Key 34). The declaration for a list in Pascal looks like this:

```
type listpointer = ^listelement;
type listelement = record
                     data: ...any data type...
                     next: listpointer
                   end;
```

List elements: To create a list element, call new(x), where x is a listpointer; store an appropriate value in x^.data; and make x^.next point to the next element.

Trees: A **tree** (Figure 6 C) is like a list, but each element has two pointers instead of one. The tree in the example is a **binary tree** designed for rapid searching.
- To **insert** a name into it, start at the root.
- If the new name alphabetically precedes the name found there, follow the left pointer; otherwise follow the right pointer.
- Keep doing this until you find a null pointer; then create a new element, store the new name in it, and hang it there.

Retrieval: Names can be **retrieved** by the same procedure, and on the average, finding a name in an *n*-element tree takes only slightly more than $\log_2 n$ steps — much faster than searching the whole tree. (Compare **binary search**, Key 41). Naturally, instead of just names, the tree can store large records or any kind of data.

Balancing: There are techniques for **balancing** a tree to make sure it has an approximately equal number of left and right branches. An unbalanced tree might have a long string of right pointers with nothing on the left, or vice versa, and this would slow down the process of searching it.

Recursion and binary trees: A binary tree is a **recursive data structure** because each tree consists of one element, plus two more trees (the left and right **subtrees**). Some of the subtrees are **empty (null)**.

KEY EXAMPLE

A recursive algorithm to print out all the names in the tree, in alphabetical order

(1) Print out the left subtree (unless it is empty).
(2) Print out the element at the root.
(3) Print out the right subtree (unless it is empty).

The key idea is that this recursive algorithm processes each subtree the same way it processes the main tree. That is, it calls itself recursively to process each subtree.

FIGURE 6

A. Linked list

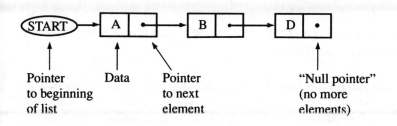

Pointer to beginning of list   Data   Pointer to next element   "Null pointer" (no more elements)

B. Inserting an element without moving any pre-existing elements

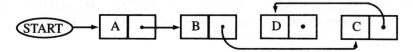

C. Binary tree designed for efficient search

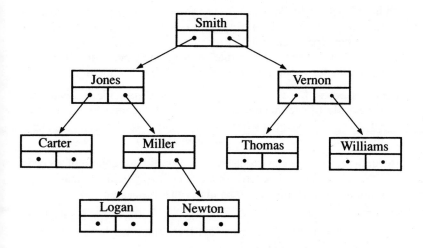

Key 46 File structures

OVERVIEW *Data structures such as lists and trees can exist on disk as well as in memory. To see how, we must review basic file structures. The main kinds of file are sequential (text and binary), random-access (direct-access), and indexed.*

Sequential files: Most files are **sequential**, which means that they are read and written one element at a time, in sequence. When the file is first **opened** (accessed from a program), the computer is ready to read at the beginning. After reading each element, the computer is ready to read the next one. Sequential files can exist on either disk or tape.

Types of sequential files:
- A **text file** is a stream of characters divided into lines, ready to be sent to the screen or printer. The end of each line is marked by ASCII 10 (UNIX) or ASCII 13 + 10 (MS-DOS). On IBM mainframes, there is no end-of-line mark; instead, the length of each line is stored as a number with the line.
- A **binary file** contains, one after another, the computer's internal binary representations of data. *Example:* To store the number 1.23 on a binary file, the computer need not convert it into the characters "1.23"; it can simply write the binary internal representation of 1.23 onto the file.

"File of type": In Pascal, a binary file of floating-point numbers is declared as f i l e o f r e a l. There could equally well be a f i l e o f any other type, even arrays or records. The important thing is that all the data items on the binary file are the same type; if they were not, the computer would not know how many bits each item occupies.

Random-access files: The alternative to a sequential file is a **random-access file (direct-access file)**, in which the computer can read or write any element at any time (for example, "read the 10th element, then write this data into the 14th element...").

Records: Such a file can reside only on disk. It must consist of **records** of equal length; each record can consist of many **fields**. In many ways a random-access file is like an **array** that resides on disk.

Use: The records in a random-access file can of course contain the locations of other records. In this way, **trees** and other linked structures can reside in disk files.

Indexed files: An **indexed** file has its records in an arbitrary order but is accompanied by another file called the **index** in which locations of records can be looked up.

Advantages: The index can be sorted without moving the records in the file itself. Also, the same file can have multiple indexes on different **keys** (e.g., a mailing list could be indexed by name and also by ZIP code).

Key 47 Relational databases

OVERVIEW *A **relational database** is a systematic way of storing information in tables of rows and columns, such that one table can refer to another and some basic operations (described below) are possible.*

Databases: A **database** is a collection of data residing on one or more files. When we talk about databases, we are talking about the structure of the data and the ways it can be retrieved, rather than the software that implements it. Many commercial database software packages exist, such as **DB2** for IBM mainframes, and **dBase III** and **Paradox** for PC's.

Relational databases: A **relational** database consists of (or is viewed as) **tables** each of which has **rows** and **columns.** *Example:*

Name	City	Salary
J. Jones	Atlanta	25,000
S. Smith	Dallas	45,000
E. Elson	Baltimore	32,000
B. Brown	Toronto	48,000

Tables: The table defines a **relation** between the items in it: J. Jones goes with Atlanta and 25,000, S. Smith goes with Dallas and 45,000, etc.

Tuples: More formally, the table is a set of **tuples** such as <*J. Jones, Atlanta, 25,000*>. A tuple is a set of values each with its particular meaning, in this case name, city, and salary.

Operations on relational databases:
- Given a table, you can **select** particular rows (such as the employees with salaries over 30,000) while discarding the rest.
- Or you can **project** particular columns (keep those columns while discarding the rest).
- If you have two tables whose columns have the same meanings, you can combine the tables to form their **union.** *Example:* The names and addresses of eastern employees could be combined with the names and addresses of western employees.
- To **join** two tables is to form a table containing information from some columns in one table and some columns in the other. *Example:* Suppose you have a table of names and addresses, plus a table of names and phone numbers. You can join these to make a table

of names, addresses, and phone numbers. In this example the person's name is the **key** that identifies which row in one table goes with which row in the other.

Structured Query Language (SQL): The purpose of the database is to answer queries. Many relational databases use **Structured Query Language (SQL)**; using the same language makes it easier for different computers to exchange data. In SQL, almost every data retrieval operation is called SELECT (including projecting and joining as defined above).

KEY EXAMPLE

An SQL query

```
SELECT NAME, SALARY FROM TABLE1
WHERE SALARY > 35000
```

Assuming TABLE1 is the table above, this query retrieves the following data:

Name	Salary
S. Smith	45,000
B. Brown	48,000

Key 48 Data compression

OVERVIEW *Data compression comprises techniques for making files, messages, or other collections of data shorter. Data compression is a matter of **trading time for space** because it takes time to decode compressed data.*

Run-length encoding: The simplest kind of data compression is **run-length encoding**. Long strings (**runs**) of repeated characters (or bits) are replaced by codes that say, "The following character is repeated N times." *Example:* In place of 200 asterisks, you could write "\200*", and in place of 53 plus signs, "\053+".

Escape characters: This encoding scheme would use \ as an **escape character** to indicate that a run-length code is coming, followed by a three-digit number and the repeated character itself.

- Normally you wouldn't encode a run unless it was at least 6 characters long. But when the character \ occurred in the input, you could encode it as "\001\" (i.e., a run of just one \) to keep it from being mistaken for an escape character.
- Of course, in place of a 3-digit number, you could use a single character and let its ASCII code (Key 5) be its numeric value; this would make the code even more efficient.

Huffman coding: A more powerful way to compress data is to **use shorter codes for the more common sequences** of characters or bits, and use longer codes for the less common ones.

KEY EXAMPLE

In this book, the word *computer* is very common, and the word *ox* is very rare. If you replaced every occurrence of *computer* with *ox* and every occurence of *ox* with *computer,* the book would be shorter. You could replace any number of common long words with uncommon short ones in the same way. Of course you'd have to maintain a table of what words had been replaced with what. If you did this with bit sequences rather than words, you'd have a type of **Huffman code**.

Bit sequences: Huffman codes represent characters or other units with bit sequences of different lengths—2 or 3 bits for the most common characters, and as many bits as necessary to distinguish the others.

Choice of sequences: The bit sequences are chosen so that none of them matches the beginning of any other. Thus if 011 is one of the codes, 0111 cannot be used, but 1011 can. This makes it possible for the computer to tell where one code ends and the next one begins.

Limitations: There is an absolute limit to how short a message can be made. To distinguish 2^n different messages, you need at least n bits.

- A file of random bits is hard or impossible to compress.
- ASCII text files can usually be compressed to 60% of their original size with Huffman codes.
- Graphic images (**bitmaps**, Key 62) can often be shrunk tremendously by run-length encoding.

Theme 8 COMPLEXITY AND COMPUTABILITY

*O*ne of the most important concerns of computer science is the power of computers. **Complexity theory** studies the number of steps required for a computation, and in particular the way this number grows with the size of the input. **Computability theory** studies limits on the power of all conceivable computers.

Key 49 Orders of complexity

OVERVIEW *In Keys 41–43 we observed informally that some algorithms take "time proportional to n^2" or "time proportional to $n \log_2 n$".* **Complexity theory** *is the branch of computer science that studies the time and space requirements of algorithms in detail.*

"Big-O" notation: Suppose the number of steps required by a particular algorithm is $f(n) = n^3 + 5n^2 + 6n + 230$ where n is the size of the input.
- If n is sufficiently large, n^3 is much larger than $5n^2$ or $6n$ or 230.
- The term n^3 **dominates** the others, and for sufficiently large n, the other terms do not matter.
- More precisely, $f(n)$ is **asymptotically bounded** by kn^3. That is, for some constant k, and for all n greater than some minimum value, kn^3 will always be greater than $f(n)$.
- Let $O(n^3)$ denote the set of functions asymptotically bounded by kn^3.
- Then $f(n) \in O(n^3)$— or, as it is more commonly but less precisely written, $f(n) = O(n^3)$. We say that $f(n)$ has **order of n^3 complexity**.

Some examples:
- Algorithms of order $O(n)$ take **linear time**.
- Orders $O(n^2)$, $O(n^3)$, $O(n^4)$, etc., take **polynomial time**.
- Linear- and polynomial-time algorithms are generally considered **tractable** (practical to compute; see Key 50).
- An algorithm that always takes the same amount of time regardless of n (**constant time**) is $O(1)$.
- You can identify the complexity of a polynomial-time algorithm by looking at the way it uses loops. A single loop with $O(n)$ steps take $O(n)$ time. One such loop within another takes $O(n^2)$ time, and so on. Be sure to look for "hidden loops" such as string searches or calls to subroutines that take non-constant time.
- An algorithm that divides the problem in half, then applies recursively to each half, will take $O(n \log_2 n)$ time.
- **Intractable** algorithms take **exponential time**, $O(k^n)$. For sufficiently large n and any constant k, k^n increases much faster than n^k.
- Note also that $1+2+3+\ldots+n$ is $O(n^2)$, and $1 \times 2 \times 3 \times \ldots \times n = n!$ is $O(k^n)$ or, equivalently, $O(e^n)$.

Key 50 NP-completeness

OVERVIEW *Some problems, such as the **traveling sales-man problem**, appear to take exponential time. Problems in this class are described as **NP-complete**, and if a polynomial-time solution is found for any of them, it will apply to all of them.*

The traveling salesman problem: Suppose you want to know the short-est path that will take you to each of n cities in any order. This is the **traveling salesman problem**. As far as is known, the only way to solve this problem is to actually enumerate all the routes and compare their lengths.

Shortcuts: There are some shortcuts — for example, you can immedi-ately abandon any route, without pursuing it to the end, as soon as you see that it is longer than the best route found so far. But these shortcuts do not change the **order of complexity** of the problem (Key 49).

Intractability: The traveling salesman problem is **intractable** because, for any n cities, the number of routes to be compared is n-**factorial** ($n! = 1 \times 2 \times 3 \times \ldots \times n$). This means the problem requires **exponential time**, $O(e^n)$. *Example:*

Number of cities, n	Number of routes, $n!$
5	120
10	3,628,800
15	1.3×10^{12}
20	2.4×10^{18}

(If 20-factorial doesn't look like a big number to you, imagine a com-puter that could do all the calculations for a route in just one microsec-ond, far faster than any computer that exists today. Evaluating routes for 20 cities would then take 1.8 million years.)

The sets P and NP: The traveling salesman problem apparently does not belong to the set **P (problems soluble in polynomial time)**. However, it does belong to the set **NP ("nondeterministic-polynomial")**, which comprises problems for which a solution can be **tested**, though not discovered, in polynomial time.

* No one has actually proved that P ≠ NP.
* However, the traveling salesman problem is known to be **NP-complete**, i.e., equivalent to the hardest problems in NP. This means that it does not belong to P unless *all* members of NP belong to P.

Other NP-complete problems:
* **bin packing** (finding the best way to arrange boxes of different sizes in a truck so that the maximum amount of cargo fits in)
* **task scheduling** (scheduling tasks of various lengths for a fixed number of workers so that the work is done as quickly as possible)
* some problems related to **finding solutions to formulas in formal logic**.

Imperfect solutions: When faced with these problems, we usually have to settle for **imperfect solutions** from algorithms that work in polynomial time but do not always find the very best solution.

Key 51   Turing machines and the halting problem

OVERVIEW   *A **Turing machine**, developed by Alan Turing (1912-1954), is an imaginary machine that serves as a mathematical model of a real computer with its program. A Turing machine consists of a processor with a finite number of **internal states**, plus a paper **tape** divided into blocks or **cells**, each of which contains one symbol chosen from a finite set of possible symbols.*

How a Turing machine works: The internal states are like instruction codes that control how the machine responds to input.

- After reading one cell from the tape, the machine will either write something back onto the tape, or move the tape one step left or right.
- Then it will go into another specified internal state or halt.
- The tape can be infinitely long; it serves as the input, output, and memory for the machine.

Church's Thesis: Proposed by Alonzo Church, the hypothesis that Turing machines do indeed have the same computational power as any imaginable digital computer. This seems reasonable because no way has been found to make Turing machines more powerful. Adding additional tapes or other mechanisms does not expand the range of computations that the machine can perform.

The halting problem: Using Turing machines, it can be proven that there is **no general solution for the halting problem** — that is, there can never be a computer program that can *always* tell you whether another program will terminate.

- Obviously, you can prove that *some* programs terminate (just run them and watch them do it), and you can prove that some other programs go into infinite loops (watch them and see that nothing is changing). But there will always be cases where you can do neither.

Proof that there is no general solution to the halting problem:

- Suppose you had a program Q that could read another program W as input, and tell you whether W halts. (By ''program'' we mean, where context requires it, ''program together with its input data,'' and we reserve the right to make a finite number of copies of it as needed.)

- Then, using Q as a subroutine, you could construct a program S that reads W and halts if W does not halt, or goes into an infinite loop if W halts. That is, S halts if and only if its input, W, does not halt.
- Now feed S a copy of itself (let W=S).
- Then S halts if and only if S does not halt, which is a contradiction. Hence S cannot exist. The only part of S that is questionable is its subroutine Q. Hence Q cannot exist.

Key 52 Formal languages and automata

OVERVIEW *A **formal language** is a set of strings of symbols. The symbols need not have meanings; a formal language is not a system of communication. Rather, the strings of symbols usually represent successive actions performed by a machine (an **automaton**; plural, **automata**).*

Generating infinite sets: An **infinite set** of strings can be described by giving a **set of rules** (a **grammar**) that **generates** (constructs) all and only the strings in the language. The nature of the rules indicates the computational power needed to create the strings.

Finite-state grammars: The simplest formal languages are generated by **finite-state grammars** (FSGs). An FSG is like a machine with a finite number of states. The machine starts in a particular state, and from each state can go to specific other states, outputting a symbol as it does so.

Memory: Such a machine has **no memory** except that it knows which state it is in at any moment. *Example:* Consider now the formal language $\{ab, aabb, aaabbb, aaaabbbb...\}$ (called $a^n b^n$ for short), in which each string has some number of a's followed by an equal number of b's An FSG cannot generate this language, because when it starts generating b's it has no way to remember how many a's it previously generated.

Context-free phrase-structure grammars: To generate $a^n b^n$ we need a **context-free phrase-structure grammar** (CF-PSG) consisting of **context-free rewrite rules** each of which rewrites one string as another.

- In addition to the **terminal symbols** a and b, which appear in the language, we also use the **non-terminal** symbol S. The rules are:
  $$S \rightarrow ab$$
  $$S \rightarrow aSb$$
- That is: Anywhere an S appears in the string, it can be **rewritten** as either ab or aSb. (The grammar is called **context-free** because it does not care what context surrounds the symbol that is being rewritten.)
- The **starting symbol** in this grammar is S. To generate $aaabbb$, we rewrite S as aSb, then $aaSbb$, then $aaabbb$.
- A CF-PSG is equivalent to a computer with a single **pushdown stack** for memory (a **pushdown automaton**).

More powerful grammars: Even context-free phrase-structure grammars cannot generate $a^n b^n c^n$ or numerous other languages. For this we need **unrestricted (context-sensitive) rewrite rules**, which have the power of a Turing machine.

Transformational grammars: Noam Chomsky and other linguists have used formal language theory to investigate the grammar of human languages (English, French, etc.), usually using **transformational grammars**, which are CF-PSGs extended with additional types of rules. (See Key 71.)

Theme 9 NUMERICAL METHODS

*N*umerical methods are techniques for using computers to solve mathematical problems with numbers. These include not only straightforward calculation, but also numerical equation solving (by successive approximations), interpolation, simulation, and statistical tests.

Key 53   Paradoxes of computer
arithmetic

OVERVIEW   *The accuracy of computer arithmetic is limited by the finite number of digits and by the fact that some numbers have no exact binary representation, and hence are subject to rounding error.*

Rounding error: Try the following calculation on your computer:

        x := 0.9 + 0.1; writeln(x);

In Turbo Pascal on an IBM PS/2, x comes out as 1.0000000001. This happens because of **rounding error**. The number 1/10 (=0.1) has **no exact binary equivalent**, and neither do most other decimal numbers.

Conversion: Try to express 1/3 as a decimal number. 0.333333 is close; 0.33333333333333 is closer; but no finite number of digits will equal 1/3 exactly. The same problem arises when the computer converts 0.1 into binary. A correct conversion would require an unlimited number of digits.

Exact equality: On the computer, $0.1 + 0.9 \neq 1.0$. The moral: **never test for exact equality** of floating-point numbers that result from computation. Instead, test whether they are sufficiently close together.

Acceptability: Some rounding error is acceptable in scientific computing, but financial work requires exactness; you would not want to lose a fraction of a cent every time you paid a bill. Financial computing often uses **BCD (binary-coded decimal) arithmetic**, in which the computer works with representations of decimal digits.

Significant digits: Other problems arise from the **limited number of significant digits** available on the computer.
- In arithmetic, $A+(B+C) = (A+B)+C$.
- But suppose $A = 0.000001$, $B = 1000$, and $C = -1000$.
- Then, on the computer, $A+(B+C) = 0.000001$, as expected.
- But $(A+B)+C$ causes a problem: $0.000001 + 1000 = 1000.000001$, which may get **truncated** to 1000.000 if not enough digits are available.
- Then adding -1000 gives 0, and the original value of A is totally lost. As a result, $(A+B)+C$ does not come out the same as $A+(B+C)$.

Key 54   Numerical equation solving

OVERVIEW   *People normally solve equations analytically, by manipulating formulas. Some equations cannot be solved this way. The computer can still solve them numerically, by successive approximations.*

Analytic equation solving: The equation $x + 2 = 2x$ can be solved by subtracting x from both sides, then simplifying $2x - x$ to x, giving $x = 2$. But some equations have **no analytic solution.** *Example:* $x = \sin x - 7$. There is no way to get x by itself on one side of the equal sign and an expression not containing x on the other side.

Numerical equation solving: Such equations can only be solved **numerically**, by trying numbers until the solution is found, or by adding up a converging series. Sometimes it is preferable to solve an equation numerically even when an analytic solution is available.

The secant method: One way to solve equations numerically is the **secant method.** To solve $x^4 = x - 7$, for example, define a function

$$f(x) = x^4 - (x - 7)$$

- That is, define $f(x)$ as the **difference between the two sides of the original equation.**
- Then try to make $f(x) = 0$.
- To do this, evaluate $f(x)$ with two arbitrarily chosen values of x (perhaps 1 and 2) and look at the results. One of them will be closer to 0 than the other, and the difference between them will tell you where to move to get even closer to 0.

Limitations: The secant method is not perfect; sometimes `f(oldx)=f(newx)`, and hence `slope=0`, leading to division by zero. Sometimes `slope` takes on values that are misleading and cause the next approximation to be a long way away from the true solution. There are many other numerical methods for solving equations.

KEY EXAMPLE

Secant method algorithm in Pascal

```
oldx := 1;
oldf := f(oldx);
newx := 2;
newf := f(newx);
repeat
 slope := (newf-oldf)/(newx-oldx);
 oldx := newx;
 newx := newx - newf/slope;
 oldf := newf;
 newf := f(newx);
 writeln(newx:15:8,newf:15:8)
until abs(newx-oldx) < 0.00001
```

Key 55 Symbolic equation solving

OVERVIEW *A computer can simplify a formula such as $x + 5 = 2x - 4$ to $5 = x - 4$ and then to $9 = x$ purely by manipulating the formula, just as people do. This is known as **symbolic equation solving**.*

Special software:
- The most famous symbolic equation solver is a program called **MACSYMA**, developed at MIT in the 1960s and still in use. MACSYMA handles basic algebra and trigonometry and can even find integrals using a large built-in table and a number of rules.
- **Mathematica**, a more modern software package for mathematicians, supports both symbolic and numerical equation solving.

How it's done: Symbolic equation solving requires **pattern matching**—the equation being solved has to be compared to stored patterns in order to decide how to handle it. For example, $x^2 + x + 3$ matches the pattern $ax^2 + bx + c$.

Use of trees: Symbolic equation solvers usually represent equations not as character strings but as **trees** (Key 45) that show the structure of the equation (Figure 7). This is easiest to do in **symbolic programming languages** such as Lisp (Key 67) and Prolog (Key 68), which can treat formulas as data. Prolog also has pattern matching built in.

FIGURE 7
Representing an equation as a tree

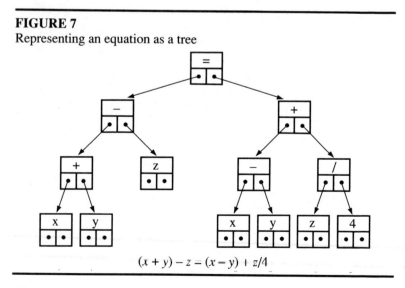

$$(x + y) - z = (x - y) + z/4$$

Key 56 Interpolation

OVERVIEW *Interpolation is the fitting of a smooth curve to a set of points (Figure 8). This is necessary either to draw a graph, or to fill in missing values in a table. For instance, if you knew the time taken by a chemical reaction at 15°C, 20°C, and 25°C, you could use interpolation to estimate the time at 23°C.*

FIGURE 8

Interpolation creates a smooth curve to connect a set of points.

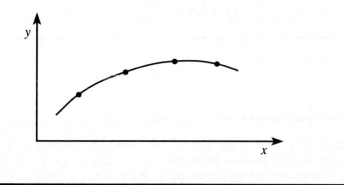

Lagrangian interpolation: For any set of *n* points, there is an (*n* − 1)-degree polynomial whose graph passes right through them. This polynomial is used in **Lagrangian interpolation**, a technique that works well when there are only four or five points and the interpolated values fall between them.

KEY EXAMPLE

Lagrangian interpolation in Pascal

Here $(x[1],y[1])...(x[n],y[n])$ are the known points; ux is the *x*-value for the unknown point, and uy is the *y*-value to be found.

```
uy := 0;
for k:=1 to n do
 begin
  p1:=1;
  p2:=1;
  for j:=1 to n do
   if j<>k then
    begin
     p1 := p1*(ux-x[j]);
     p2 := p2*(x[k]-x[j])
    end;
  uy := uy + y[k]*p1/p2
end;
```

Limitations: With larger numbers of points, Lagrangian interpolation produces a rather lumpy curve; also, the Lagrangian curve tends to go sharply up or down at the ends. For best results, use Lagrangian interpolation with 4 known points, two above and two below the unknown point.

Alternatives: More natural-looking curves can be obtained with **cubic spline interpolation**. With cubic splines, each segment of the curve is influenced only by the two points that it connects, plus the slopes of the two adjacent segments that it links to.

Key 57 Random numbers

OVERVIEW *Many computer simulations and games use* ***random numbers***. *Nothing is truly "random" (unpredictable) on a properly functioning computer. Numbers are considered random if they* ***follow no discernible pattern*** *(or at least no pattern related to what they are being used for) and are* ***evenly distributed*** *(so that each has an equal probability of occurring).*

Random numbers: Seemingly random numbers are common in mathematics. *Example:* Look at the middle digits of a function such as sine, cosine, or square root:

x	$\sin x$
1°	0.017**452**406
2°	0.034**899**496
3°	0.052**335**956
4°	0.069**756**473

The first digits (0.017, 0.034, etc.) are non-random since they reflect the value of the function. The rightmost digits are unevenly distributed because of inaccuracy. The middle digits (shown in boldface) are effectively random.

A more practical algorithm: A faster way to get random numbers is to pick an arbitrary integer k (the **seed**) and repeatedly compute:

```
k := (k*106 + 1283) mod 6075
```

- This makes k take on seemingly random values from 0 and 6074 inclusive.
- The coefficients 106, 1283, and 6075 are carefully chosen so that the sequence of numbers does not repeat until the 6075th iteration.

Using the random number generator:
- To get **random floating-point numbers** from 0 to 1, use $k/6074$.
- To get **random integers in a smaller range** 0 to n-1, use k modulo n (where n is much less than 6074).

Unguessable numbers: This formula produces the same random numbers each time you use it with the same seed. To get **unguessable numbers** for games and the like, start k with a number obtained from the system clock, such as the time of day in milliseconds.

Limitations: This kind of formula is called a **linear congruential generator**. Note that it uses large integers; in this example, k*106 can be as high as 643,844, too bit to fit into a 16-bit integer. Most programming languages have a **built-in random number generator** that works around this problem by breaking the multiplication and modulo operations into intermediate steps.

Key 58 Simulation

OVERVIEW *To **simulate** something is to model its internal workings on the computer. This is often done to study processes that are too complex to analyze mathematically.*

KEY EXAMPLE

A simulation

Suppose you want to know the best way to time the traffic lights in a small town.

After collecting data on the number and speed of cars in each direction, how quickly they accelerate when the light turns green, etc., you *could* try to derive a mathematical formula to give the optimum traffic light timing. But this could be immensely difficult.

A simpler approach would be to **model** the streets and traffic lights on the computer:

- Write a program that keeps track of the positions of cars on an imaginary set of streets just like the real ones.
- Introduce imaginary cars with known, realistic behavior, and calculate what their positions would be every few seconds.
- Run many simulations with different traffic light timings until the traffic moves the way you want it to.

Calculating probabilities by simulation: Simulation is also useful to calculate **probabilities** of events that are **complex combinations of many causes**.

KEY EXAMPLE

Finding probabilities by simulation

Suppose for example you are manufacturing radios. Each radio has perhaps 100 components, each of which has a known probability of being out of tolerance (actually, a known **distribution**, Key 57). Sometimes, variations in components don't matter, and sometimes they even cancel each other out.

Given the probabilities that each component will be out of tolerance, what is the probability that the whole radio will not work? Again, you could try to derive the probability mathematically, but simulation is easier.

- Randomly choose a set of characteristics for all of the parts, then calculate whether the radio works. Do this again with another set of randomly chosen parts, and another, and another.
- Make sure that the random values for each simulated component have the same statistical distribution as the values for the corresponding real component.
- Then the fraction of simulated radios that work will be a good estimate of the fraction of real radios that work.

Monte Carlo methods: Simulation can even be used to solve purely mathematical problems. In this case simulations are called **Monte Carlo methods** (Monte Carlo is a gambling resort).

KEY EXAMPLE

Finding an integral by Monte Carlo methods

Suppose for example that you want to find the area of an irregularly shaped figure.

Suppose further that you have no analytic way to find the area, but you do have an easy way to test whether any particular point is within or outside the figure. Then here's how to proceed.

- Draw a rectangle around the irregular shape, then choose random points within that rectangle.
- As you use more and more random points, the fraction of them that fall in the irregular shape will give you a better and better indication of what fraction of the rectangle is filled by the shape.
- The points have to be random so that you can be sure that their distribution will not have any special relationship to the irregularly shaped figure that you are trying to investigate.

Key 59 Statistics that summarize data

OVERVIEW *Statistics such as the **mean**, **median**, **mode**, **variance**, and **standard deviation** are ways of describing, with just a few numbers, the distribution of a large number of measured values.*

Distribution: Figure 9 shows a **histogram** of the scores of an imaginary exam on which everyone scored between 90 and 100. The shape of the histogram represents the **distribution** of values.

Types: This particular distribution is **unimodal** (one-peaked; if it had two peaks it would be **bimodal**). In fact this histogram is almost perfectly **Gaussian ("normal," bell-curve-shaped)**—the distribution that is expected when each value is the **sum** of many random variables.

FIGURE 9

Histogram of imaginary exam scores

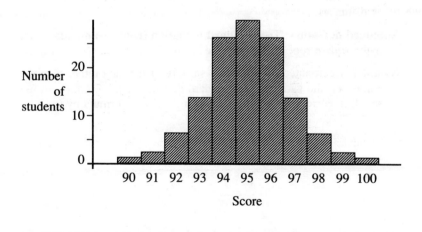

Measures of central tendency:

- The **mean ("average")** is the sum of the values, divided by the number of values. Thus, for n values $A_1...A_n$,

$$mean = (A_1 + A_2 + ... + A_n)/n$$

- The **median** is the value that has an equal number of other values above it and below it.
- The **mode** is the value that occurs most often (the peak in the histogram).

Effects of distribution: In a perfectly Gaussian distribution, the mean, median, and mode are the same. But the mean is excessively affected by **non-Gaussian distribution** and especially by **outliers** (values far away from the mean). Suppose one student had scored 20 instead of 91. This would lower the mean quite a bit, but the mode and median are not affected at all.

Measures of deviation: The **variance** (σ^2) tells how wide the peak is— whether all the values are bunched close to the mean or whether they are far away from it:

$$variance = [(A_1-mean)^2 + (A_2-mean)^2 + ... + (A_n-mean)^2]/n$$

You can think of the variance as a kind of average of the distance from each value to the mean.

- We square the distances to make them all positive so they don't cancel each other out.
- Squaring also makes one big distance count more than two small distances.

Standard deviation: The **standard deviation (root-mean-square, σ)** is the square root of the variance.

Sample: If computed on a random **sample** of the data rather than the whole set, the variance and standard deviation tend to come out too small; to correct for this, replace n in the above formula by $(n - 1)$.

Key 60   Statistics that test hypotheses

OVERVIEW   *The statistics in Key 59 merely **summarize** data. Statistics are also used to **test hypotheses** (for example, does high cholesterol cause heart disease?). The crucial problem here is **inference from a sample**. You cannot examine all the people who have high cholesterol, merely a sample of them.*

How to analyze a sample:
- The first question is whether the sample is **fair**, i.e., typical of the population. Unfortunately, no mathematical test can tell you this.
- The next question is whether two things are **correlated** in the sample. That is, is heart disease more common among people in the sample who have high cholesterol than among the other people in the sample? If so, high cholesterol and heart disease are **positively correlated**.
- The third question is whether the correlation is **significant**. That is, does it reflect a correlation in the population as a whole, or is it just an effect of sampling? After all, the incidence of heart disease in two randomly chosen groups of people will almost never be *exactly* the same. A sample is only a sample.

Significance: Significance is measured relative to a **confidence level**. "Significant at **the .05 level**" (sometimes called **.95 level**) means there is only a 5% chance, or less, that the correlation is an illusion caused by sampling.

Tests: Several **significance tests** are in common use. The **chi-square test** tells you whether several alternative outcomes have the predicted set of probabilities. The **t test** tells you whether the means of two different populations are the same (even though the means of the samples are different).

Size vs. significance: Significant differences should not be confused with **large differences**. Suppose something raises a person's chance of heart disease from 0.06 to 0.0600001. With a gigantic sample, this could be a *significant* difference, but it is definitely not *large*.

Certainty: Remember, too, that **significance is not certainty**. If you find 100 things to be significant at the .05 level, then on the average, about 5 of them will nonetheless be illusory.

Key 61 Permutations and combinations

OVERVIEW *This is a review of some essential concepts and formulas used in calculating the number of steps in a computation.*

Permutations
- The **permutations of *n* objects** are the sequences into which *n* objects can be arranged.

KEY EXAMPLE

Permutations of *n* objects

Suppose there are 12 objects. When you choose the one to put first, you have 12 to choose from. After each of these, you then have 11 choices for what to put next, then 10 choices of what to put after that, and so on. So the number of permutations is

$$P(12) = 12 \times 11 \times 10 \times 9 \times 8 \times 7 \times 6 \times 5 \times 4 \times 3 \times 2 \times 1$$

or more generally,

$$P(n) = n \times (n\text{-}1) \times (n\text{-}2) \times \ldots \times 3 \times 2 \times 1 = n!$$

where *n*! denotes *n*-factorial.

- The **permutations of *n* objects taken *m* at a time** are the sequences in which you can arrange the first *m* objects that you choose from a set of *n*.

KEY EXAMPLE

Pemutations of *n* objects taken *m* at a time

Suppose you want to choose any 8 out of a set of 12. Then the formula is like the one above, but only the first 8 choices count!

$$P(12,8) = 12 \times 11 \times 10 \times 9 \times 8 \times 7 \times 6 \times 5$$

Think of this as P(12) except that the sequence of the last 4 elements does not count because those elements are not chosen. So P(12) should be divided by the number of sequences that we are treating alike in each case:

$$P(12,8) = P(12)/P(4)$$

$$P(n,m) = P(n)/P(n\text{-}m) = n!/(n\text{-}m)!$$

Combinations: Combinations are like permutations except that order doesn't count at all.

KEY EXAMPLE

Combinations of *n* objects taken *m* at a time

In this case, if you're picking 8 elements from a set of 12, you don't care about the order of the 8 elements that you choose, nor the order of the 4 that you don't choose.

So C(12,8) will be P(12) divided by P(8) and also divided by P(4):

$$C(12,8) = P(12)/(P(8) \times P(4)) = 12!/(8! \times 4!)$$

$$C(n,m) = n!/(m! \times (n\text{-}m)!)$$

Subsets: Finally, any *n*-element set has 2^n **subsets**. The set of all subsets of a set is called its **power set**.

Theme 10 COMPUTER GRAPHICS

*C*omputer graphics is the creation and manipulation of pictures or images by the computer. An image usually represented as an array of **pixels** (picture elements). Computer graphics includes not only the generation of images by computer, but also the computer processing of pictures from other sources.

Key 62   Basic graphics

OVERVIEW   *Vector and raster representations are used to create and display images on the computer.*

Vector graphics: In **vector graphics**, the output device draws a smooth line between two points; the whole image is a combination of such lines. Vector graphics is used with **pen plotters** that draw on paper with a pen.

Raster graphics: Computer screens and printers, however, use **raster graphics**, in which the image is an array of dots called **pixels (pels)** (Figure 10), numbered with x and y **coordinates**.

Resolution: The **resolution** of the display is the number of pixels available (1024×1024 on modern workstations, 320×200 on low-cost home computers).

Printers: These usually have gigantic resolution (e.g., 300 **dots per inch**, or 2400×3000 on an 8×10-inch printout), but this is no advantage if the program prints the same pixels that are shown on the screen.

FIGURE 10

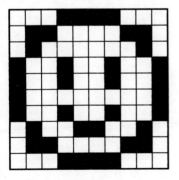

```
0 0 0 1 1 1 1 0 0 0
0 1 1 0 0 0 0 1 1 0
0 1 0 0 0 0 0 0 1 0
1 0 0 1 0 0 1 0 0 1
1 0 0 1 0 0 1 0 0 1
1 0 0 0 0 0 0 0 0 1
1 0 0 1 0 0 1 0 0 1
0 1 0 0 1 1 0 0 1 0
0 1 1 0 0 0 0 1 1 0
0 0 0 1 1 1 1 0 0 0
```

Image   Bitmap

Bitmaps: Black-and-white (**monochrome**) raster graphic images are represented in memory as **bitmaps**, with one bit indicating whether each pixel is on or off. Bitmaps are easily **compressed** with run-length encoding (Key 48).

Color internal representations: Color images use more than one bit per pixel, e.g., 4 bits per pixel for 16 colors. These are often divided into **planes** so that there in one bitmap for red, another for green, another for blue, and another for extra intensity, and all colors are made by mixing these **primary colors**.

Program vs. screen: It is common practice to use vector graphics inside a program to describe images concisely, even though the screen uses raster graphics.

Turtle graphics: Some programs use **turtle graphics**, a variant of vector graphics in which a line is drawn by a pointer that accepts instructions of the form, "Move n pixels forward... change direction n degrees to the right or left."

Paint programs and draw programs: The different advantages of vectors and bitmaps are illustrated by the two kinds of programs that allow computer users to create and edit drawings.
- **Paint programs** such as MacPaint (on the Macintosh) let the user edit the pixel array directly with tools that act like pencils, compasses, brushes, erasers, etc.
- **Draw programs** such as MacDraw do not edit the bitmap directly; instead they maintain a **linked list** (Key 45) of vector-like **objects** (lines, circles, etc.) which can be moved around independently of each other, even when they occupy overlapping pixels.

Key 63 Graphics programming

OVERVIEW *Programming languages that support graphics have a large number of built-in procedures for drawing lines, circles, and curves, and for transforming images.*

Scan conversion: A central concern of computer graphics is **scan conversion**, the creation of raster graphics from other kinds of descriptions.

Built-in routines: Most programming languages that support graphics have line- and circle-drawing routines built in. These usually use **Bresenham's algorithms,** which run fast because they use only integer arithmetic.

Filling: Another common built-in operation is **filling a closed area** with a color.

Curves: Spline curves connect points with smooth curves. Whereas **interpolation** (Key 56) requires curves that go through all the points in a set, graphic images often use **Bézier splines,** each of which connects two points and is pulled toward, but not into, other **"influence points"** along the way.

Transformations:
*   **Coordinate transformation** is the resizing or rotation of a 2- or 3-dimensional image.
*   **Projection** is the rendering of three dimensions in two. Projections are done from a specific viewing angle, with or without **perspective.** Projection usually requires **hidden-line removal** or **hidden-surface removal.** A **wire-frame image** does not attempt this, but merely draws the outline of the whole object, as if all the edges would be visible at once.

Color: In computer graphics, color is normally handled through **palettes.** A palette is a lookup table that relates color numbers (0 to 3, 0 to 15, or 0 to 255) to actual mixtures of red, green, and blue. When an entry in the palette is changed, all areas of the image whose color number is affected instantly change color.

Ray tracing: Highly realistic images of 3-dimensional objects can be generated through **ray tracing.** The computer can calculate exactly how much light would reflect off each point on the object being depicted, given the texture of the surface and the characteristics of the light source.

Key 64   Image processing

OVERVIEW   *Image processing is the manipulation of an image by computer. This is normally done to make important details more visible. For instance, the images sent back to earth by space probes are almost always computer-processed.*

Brightness: One task is to **adjust the brightness range** of the picture. This is done by constructing a **histogram** (Key 59) of the brightnesses of the pixels, then transforming the brightnesses to spread them out over the available range. This corrects a picture that is too light or too dark or has too little contrast.

Color: Color can be corrected, and **false-color** images can be produced in which colors are greatly exaggerated (as in the pink-and-blue Voyager pictures of Saturn).

Filtering: Another kind of processing is **local contrast enhancement**: make a pixel brighter if it is already brighter than the average of its neighbors, and darker if it is already darker than the average of its neighbors. This makes low-contrast detail more visible without changing the brightness range of the picture as a whole.

Fourier transform: Local contrast enhancement is actually a kind of **filtering**; implicitly, it works on a **Fourier transform** of the image. This is so because it favors details of a particular size.
- A Fourier transform translates an image into a set of **spatial frequencies** (detail sizes), just as the Fourier transform of a sound wave would translate it into a spectrum of audio frequencies. Some of these frequencies can then be amplified or suppressed before the Fourier transform is converted back into an image.
- This makes it possible to **filter out stripes**, **speckles**, and other imperfections. More sophisticated manipulations can even **refocus a blurred image**, provided the exact nature of the blur is known. This is being done to overcome optical defects in the Hubble Space Telescope.

Theme 11 ARTIFICIAL INTELLIGENCE

*A*rtificial intelligence (AI) is the modeling of human thinking by computer. Its main areas are general problem solving, automated reasoning, expert systems, natural language processing, robotics, computer vision, and neural networks. Most AI programming is done in the Lisp and Prolog languages.

Key 65   Can computers be intelligent?

OVERVIEW   *There has always been debate as to whether computers can ever really think, and how we might test whether they are doing so. The **Turing test** is a classic definition of intelligence as applied to machines.*

Goal: The original goal of AI was to make computers intelligent. But often, as soon as computers become able to do some particular thing (such as play chess or understand English), people stop saying that that ability constitutes "intelligence."

Turing test: In 1950, Alan Turing proposed the **Turing test (imitation game)**; if a computer, communicating only by teletype, can convince another human that it is a human being, then the computer possesses human-like intelligence.

Searle's Chinese room: In reply, philosopher John Searle offers the **Chinese room argument**.
- Suppose a person who speaks only English memorizes a large set of rules that tell him how to answer questions in Chinese. The rules do not say what the Chinese questions *mean*— they only say how to construct an answer.
- Eventually, this person should be able to pass the Turing test in Chinese even though he does not know the meanings of any Chinese words and cannot be said to understand the questions.

Intentionality: Searle's point is that human-like intelligence requires conscious awareness and intentionality, not just the ability to carry on a natural-sounding conversation. This does not prove that machines will never think; it only shows that the Turing test is not an adequate way of judging whether a machine has human-like intelligence.

Philosophical context: The Turing test is analogous to the philosophical **problem of other minds**: How do you know that people other than yourself have thoughts and feelings? For all you know, they may just be giving convincing answers to questions like the man in Searle's Chinese room. Obviously, this is a ridiculous conclusion, but disproving it is difficult.

What is intelligence? Over the years it has become obvious that **there is no single mental ability called "intelligence"** (as used to be claimed by advocates of IQ tests); instead, people have many different mental abilities. Thus, AI is a matter of modeling **many different human abilities**, not just one.

AI today: AI started out in the 1950s as the study of how to make computers think like people. But this goal may be obsolete. Today it is more accurate to say that artificial intelligence is the computer modeling of human mental abilities, for either of two purposes: to understand the human mind better or to make computers more powerful

Key 66   Solving problems by searching
trees

OVERVIEW   *Intelligent behavior often involves finding the right series of actions to reach a goal. One way to do this is to set out the choices in a* **goal tree** *(search tree, game tree) and then search the tree.*

KEY EXAMPLE

Figure 11 shows a maze, together with the same maze rearranged as a tree.

The tree diagram shows where you can go from each position provided you never back up. Similar trees could describe games of chess, checkers, etc., showing the possible moves at each stage.

To solve the maze, all you have to do is search the tree from START until you find FINISH. The important thing is that the **tree shows the structure of the problem**, and any method of solving the problem is equivalent to some form of tree search.

Depth-first search: In **depth-first search**, you follow each branch to its end, then back up to the most recent untried alternative. On the tree in Figure 11, you would visit positions 2, 1, 6, 7, 8, 13, 3, 4, 5, 9, 14, etc., in that order.

Breadth-first search: In **breadth-first search** you move forward only after trying all the alternatives at a particular level. A breadth-first search would visit positions 2, 1, 3, 6, 4, etc., in that order.

  • **To implement depth-first or breadth-first search**, keep a list of positions you are going to visit (initially just {2}, then {1,3}, etc.).

  • Visit whatever position comes first in the list. When you do so, remove it from the list and add the positions that are reachable from it in one move. For a depth-first search, add these at the beginning of the list; for a breadth-first search, add them at the end. Then visit whatever is now first in the list, and so on.

Heuristic search: A **heuristic** search strategy does not visit every node, but only the ones that seem likely to lead to a solution. With a heuristic search, you run the risk of failing to find a solution, but most of the time you will find a solution more quickly than with a complete search.

FIGURE 11

A maze and a goal tree for solving it

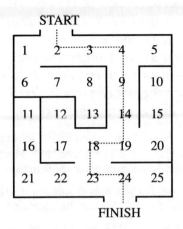

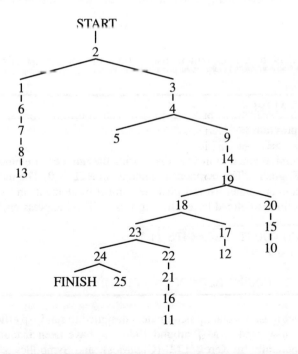

Key 67 Lisp

OVERVIEW *Most American AI research has used the programming language **Lisp** (List Processor), developed by John McCarthy around 1958. Lisp is especially suitable for AI because it is a **symbolic** language, designed to handle lists, trees, formulas, and other complex data structures, and to create them easily at run time. Lisp is also **reflexive**, which means the program can modify itself. A Lisp program can create Lisp expressions, then execute them.*

Expressions: The basic Lisp operation is to **evaluate** a **symbolic expression.** *Example:* (+ 2 3) evaluates to 5. More formally, (+ 2 3) means ''Pass 2 and 3 as arguments to the **function** whose name is +.''

Quote: The **quote** operator prevents evaluation. For instance, ' (+ 2 3) evaluates to the list (+ 2 3), not the number 5.

CAR, CDR: The functions CAR and CDR separate a list into, respectively, its first element and a list of the remaining elements. For example,

$$(CAR '(A B C)) = A$$
$$(CDR '(A B C)) = (B C)$$

The CDR of a one-element list is ( ), the empty list, also called NIL.

KEY EXAMPLE

A Lisp program

This recursive function in Lisp that counts the number of elements in a list. In English: ''The number of elements in NIL is 0. The number of elements in any other list is 1 plus the number of elements in its CDR.'' The function is defined by evaluating this DEFUN expression.

```
(DEFUN COUNT-ELEMENTS (L)
 (IF (= L NIL)
  0
  (+ 1 (COUNT-ELEMENTS (CDR L)))))
```

Lisp machines: Special minicomputers designed to run Lisp efficiently. They originated at MIT around 1980 and have been manufactured commercially by Xerox, LMI (GigaMos), and Symbolics.

Key 68 Prolog

OVERVIEW *The programming language **Prolog** (Programming in Logic) is widely used in newer AI research. It is especially well suited for **expert systems** (Key 70) and **natural language processing** (Key 71) because, in addition to being symbolic and reflexive like Lisp, it has depth-first search (Key 66) and pattern-matching (**unification**) built in.*

Programming in logic: Alain Colmerauer invented Prolog around 1974 as a computer implementation of formal logic (**"logic programming"**). A program (or **knowledge base**) consists of **clauses**, which are of two types: **facts**, which stand alone, and **rules**, which call other clauses.

KEY EXAMPLE

In Prolog, the **fact** "Michael is the father of Cathy" can be expressed as
```
father(michael,cathy).
```
and the **rule** "X is a parent of Y if X is the father of Y" is written as
```
parent(X,Y) :- father(X,Y).
```
These define the **predicates** father and parent. Given these, the Prolog system can answer the **query**
```
?-parent(michael,W).
```
by displaying the solution W=cathy.

Recursive list processing: In Prolog, matching a list with [X | Y] will make X equal to the first element and Y equal to the list of remaining elements.

KEY EXAMPLE

Here is a Prolog procedure that counts the elements of a list (compare Key 67). The procedure has two definitions; one matches the argument [ ] (the empty list) and the other matches any list that can be split into CAR and CDR.
```
count_elements([ ],0).
count_elements([X | Y],N) :-
  count_elements(Y,M),
  N is M+1.
```

Key 69 Automated reasoning

OVERVIEW *One important task of artificial intelligence is to emulate human logical reasoning. In this, AI is assisted by formal logic, the mathematical modeling of logical thinking.*

Truth-preserving inference: The key idea of logic is that some kinds of reasoning are **truth-preserving**, i.e., if you start with true **premises** (assumptions), you will certainly end up with true conclusions. *Example:* If all men are mortal and Socrates is a man, then Socrates is mortal, and you know this even if you don't know what *man* or *mortal* or *Socrates* means.

Limits: Logic cannot tell you whether the premises are true. Logic only tells you that *if* the premises are true, then the conclusions are also true.

Boolean algebra: George Boole (1815-1864) was the first to realize that logical arguments can be manipulated like mathematical formulas **(Boolean algebra)**. *Example:* From $(\forall x)man(x) \rightarrow mortal(x)$ and *man(socrates)* the rules of logic allow you to **prove** (derive) the conclusion *mortal(socrates)*.

Algorithms: Most automated reasoning systems are built around **theorem-proving algorithms**; indeed, such an algorithm is built into Prolog (Key 68).

Classical logic: It has been shown that **classical logic is incomplete**, i.e., some theorems will never be proved by any algorithm. Some other theorems are provable but are missed by particular algorithms (including Prolog's) in the interest of efficiency.

Nonclassical logics: Unlike classical formal logic, human reasoning can deal with uncertainty and exceptions.
- One way to model this on the computer is to replace the two values "true" and "false" with a continuum from 0 to 1 **(confidence factors, certainty factors, fuzzy logic)**.
- The other is to use **default reasoning (defeasible reasoning)**, in which some conclusions are drawn only tentatively and can be revised when further information is available.

Key 70 Expert systems

OVERVIEW *The most successful industrial applications of AI so far are **expert systems**, which are computer programs that give advice and draw conclusions just like a human expert. Expert systems are often used to diagnose diseases, identify defects in machines, and select products. MYCIN, an early expert system developed at Stanford University, was able to identify blood infections more reliably than human doctors.*

Why use expert systems? Although intrinsically less intelligent than a human being, an expert system has the advantages that it is:
- **consistent** (always does the same thing in the same situation);
- **easy to replicate** (you just copy disks instead of training more people);
- **able to handle a large database** without forgetting any of the information.

Components: Each expert system consists of a **knowledge base** of human like knowledge, an **inference engine** for applying this knowledge to a real-life situation, and a **user interface** for communicating with the user.

Chaining: A **forward-chaining** inference engine starts with data and tries to draw conclusions from it. A **backward-chaining** inference engine works through a set of conclusions (e.g., possible diagnoses) and determines which of them are consistent with the data.

Knowledge engineering: The knowledge base is usually built with information obtained from a human expert in the field. This process is called **knowledge engineering** and is often done through repeated interviews.

Format of knowledge base: Expert systems are **not based on flowcharts or decision trees**. The job of the inference engine is to find and apply the rules and facts that pertain to the situation at hand.

Maintainability: Expert systems should be **maintainable**. That is, it should be easy to check for errors in the knowledge base. This requires that each rule or fact should be understandable in isolation. Systems based on certainty factors (Key 69) often have trouble here, because there is no way to tell which rule will win out, in a conflict, without looking at all the other rules.

Key 71 Natural language processing

OVERVIEW *Natural language processing (NLP) is the understanding of human languages by a computer. This does not always mean the computer must think like a human; all it means is that the computer should be able to use English, French, or another human language to accept the kind of data it normally processes.*

Why NLP is hard: One difficulty with NLP is that nobody knows exactly how human languages work. The human brain is genetically pre-programmed to learn language, and children learn to talk almost automatically. Although we humans can speak languages, we cannot explain or describe how we do it.

Simple NLP systems: Template and keyword NLP systems do not try to replicate human language ability; they just recognize words and phrases in limited contexts. For many practical purposes, this is sufficient because there are only a few things the human user can say. *Example:* Suppose you want to use English as the command language for a computer. You can assume that users will talk about disks, files, etc., but not about the meaning of life.

Levels of linguistic analysis: More sophisticated NLP systems analyze language on several levels (although the levels interact):
- **Phonology** studies how speech sounds are used in a language. **Speech recognition** by computer is difficult because speech sounds overlap in time (the *a* and *n* in the word *man* are almost simultaneous) and because different people speak differently. **Speech synthesis** is much easier, though the resulting speech does not sound entirely natural.
- **Morphology** is the study of word formation (simple in English).
- **Syntax** is sentence structure. Syntactic analysis is called **parsing**; it involves breaking sentences into **constituents** (Figure 12).
- **Semantics** (meaning) and **pragmatics** (use of language in context) are much harder to computerize because they involve the relation between the language and the knowledge to be expressed in it. A big challenge is **ambiguity** (use of the same word with different meanings in different contexts).

FIGURE 12

Constituents of an English sentence

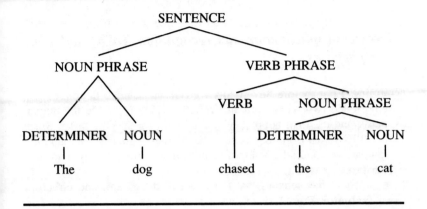

Key 72   Robotics and computer vision

OVERVIEW *A **robot** is a computer that manipulates objects or moves itself around. **Computer vision** is the recognition of objects in a digitized image (Key 64). This is used not only for robotics, but also for recognizing written characters (**optical character recognition, OCR**) and many other purposes.*

Robotics: Long before any robots were built, science fiction writers envisioned two types: **android robots**, which resemble the human body, and **usiform robots**, which are built for specific tasks. Since the 1960s, usiform robots have been used regularly for handling radioactive materials, assembling machinery automatically, and similar tasks.

- A robot has **sensors** that tell it where things are, and **effectors (actuators)** that move things.
- All but the simplest robots rely on a **feedback loop** between sensors and effectors. To move something 20 centimeters, a robot does not just blindly execute a movement 20 cm long; it moves until its sensors tell it the right position has been reached.

Computer vision: Computer vision is at least as complicated as natural language processing (NLP, Key 71) and resembles it in an important way: both computer vision and NLP try to replicate something that the human brain is genetically pre-programmed to do. In the case of vision, this pre-programming is very specialized. For example, people are especially good at recognizing human faces.

Recognizing objects: To recognize objects in images, the computer must do three things:

- **Image processing** to discard irrelevant information and make the relevant information easier to get to.
- **Pattern recognition** to identify objects (or components of objects) in the image. This can be difficult because the same object looks different when viewed from a different angle or in different light.
- **Scene analysis** to figure out how the objects fit together. This includes **perspective** (reconstruction of 3 dimensions from 2), as well as some knowledge of the physical world.

Key 73   Neural networks

OVERVIEW   *The human brain is very efficient at some things that have turned out to be very hard to do on conventional computers. This is apparently because the brain's structure is very different from a computer.* **Neural networks** *are computing techniques that simulate the internal structure of the brain.*

Theory:
- Inside the brain, nerve cells **(neurons)** are connected in such a way that each neuron has many inputs but only one output (which however can go to more than one other neuron). The strength of the output is proportional to the sum of the inputs.
- Some neuron outputs **excite**, and others **inhibit**, the neuron inputs to which they are connected. The network **learns** by adjusting the strengths of the connections so that a particular input produces a particular output.
- A neural network on the computer simulates this (Figure 13).
- Importantly, **neural networks do not presuppose a digital computer**; they could be built with analog hardware, though at present they are simulated by programs running on digital computers with floating-point arithmetic.

Practice:
- To **train** the simulated neural network, patterns are applied to the input and output.
- A simple algorithm then adjusts the **weights** of the simulated connections until the output pattern comes out right. This algorithm usually includes **backpropagation** so that the adjustments can reach neurons other than the last row.
- Simulated neural networks are strikingly good at tasks that defy conventional computerization, such as recognizing faces or other patterns.
- Like the human brain, they give **approximate rather than exact results**.
- Further, their **internal structure is not accessible** in any meaningful way. Neural networks do not contain anything like the facts or rules of an expert system. They contain large sets of numbers which are meaningless to a human being.

- It is almost impossible to predict with certainty how a neural network will behave with inputs that have not yet been presented to it. Thus neural networks will never have the reliability that we expect from conventional computer programs.

FIGURE 13

A neural network

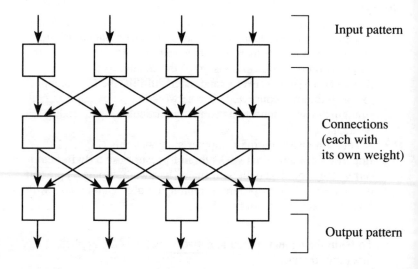

Input pattern

Connections (each with its own weight)

Output pattern

Theme 12 HUMAN ASPECTS OF
COMPUTING

*T*his theme deals with the way computers relate to human beings. This includes programmers (concerned with how to write programs reliably), computer users (concerned with using software effectively), employees (concerned with working conditions), and society as a whole.

Key 74   Designing reliable software

OVERVIEW   *Reliability of computer programs is presently a serious problem, even though computers themselves are among the most reliable machines ever built. People take it for granted that every substantial computer program will contain **errors**, which are called **bugs** as if they could creep in all by themselves. This Key gives guidelines for bug-free programming.*

Think about the problem, not about the computer: Don't just think of *one* way to solve the problem. Think of *several* ways. **Plan the algorithm** and the data structures even before you choose the programming language to use.

Use appropriate tools: Whatever makes your program shorter and simpler will make it more reliable.
- Use a **programming language** that fits the task.
- Also use **libraries** of pre-written code whenever possible.

Divide the program into sections: Limit the ways sections interact, so that you never have to understand more than about 20 lines of code at one time. Begin each section with a comment that says what it does. Write the comments *before* you write the code.

Make it readable: Use neat layout, meaningful variable names, and comments. Even you will one day forget how your program works. This can easily happen before you finish writing it!

Stop and think: Take the extra minute to convince yourself logically that your program is correct, rather than programming by trial and error. If you're not sure whether to write i<1 or i<=1, stop and figure it out. Don't rely on testing to find your errors later.

Key 75   Testing programs and proving them correct

OVERVIEW *Programs are trustworthy if we are logically certain that their algorithms are correct. Spot-checking a program with a few different inputs is no way to make sure it is error-free.*

Why do you trust your pocket calculator? Consider addition of integers.
- Your calculator can add at least 10,000,000,000,000,000 different pairs of 8-digit numbers.
- How do you know it adds them correctly? Have you tried them all? Has someone at the factory? Of course not. You trust your calculator because you believe it uses a **correct algorithm**.
- That is, whoever designed the calculator could **prove mathematically that it performs addition correctly** on all inputs. Such a proof may not have been actually written down, but the correctness of the algorithm would be obvious to anyone who studied it.

Applying the same concept to computers: Computer programs should work the same way. Since the 1960s, researchers have worked on ways of **proving programs correct**.
- Two practical results have been **dataflow analysis** (keeping track of which statements in a program affect which variables) and **structured programming** (managing flow of control so that it is easy to see what will happen, Key 30).
- The concept of proving programs correct has done a lot to make programs more reliable, even if formal proofs are not written down. The key idea is that **the correctness of a program is shown not by running it, but by reasoning logically about what it says**.

Doing things the old way: Unfortunately, most programmers follow an older tradition of testing programs as if they were machines, i.e., **writing unreliable programs and then randomly spot-checking for misbehavior.** ("Run it and see if it works.")
- The trouble with spot-checking is that **no one will ever test more than a few of the inputs that the program is supposed to process.**

- Reliance on this kind of testing condemns the program to be forever unreliable.

Testing: Program testing is usually divided into **alpha-testing** (by the manufacturer) and **beta-testing** (by selected users). This kind of testing is essential and should be done extensively, but catching errors is no substitute for preventing them.

Key 76 User interfaces

OVERVIEW   *The **user interface** of a computer program is the part of it that communicates with the user. More than anything else, the user interface determines whether the program will be easy to use.*

Desirable qualities:
- A good user interface should be **understandable and intuitive**; it should let the user think about the problem to be solved, not about the computer.
- As far as possible, the user should **not have to learn new terms or concepts** before using the program.
- A good user interface should also be **similar to user interfaces for other**, **similar programs** so that users can apply the computer knowledge they already have. (Exactly duplicating another program's user interface can, however, violate copyright; Key 78.)

Command languages: For expressing commands or describing data. If designed systematically, a command language can be powerful and relatively easy to remember, but time-consuming to type.

Keystrokes: Editors and spreadsheets usually use **special keystrokes** for specific actions (e.g., Ctrl-Y to delete a line). This is practical only if most of the keys are **used very frequently**, or else the user cannot remember them.

Menus: An especially popular kind of user interface. In a **bounce bar menu**, the user moves a colored bar up and down to select an item. Other menus let the user choose items by typing numbers or letters.
- A particularly good way to make menu choices is to **type the first letter** of the word being chosen (e.g., R for Run, E for Edit). This is not as error-prone as typing arbitrary numbers or moving a bounce bar.
- One problem with menus is **menu navigation:** the user may not know which menu contains the item he wants to choose, or how to get to it. Systematic design overcomes this.

Graphic user interfaces: Graphical operating systems such as that of the Macintosh (Key 23) provide a **graphical user interface** for all programs. Menus look alike, and work similarly, for all software on the computer; as a result, learning to use a new program is not a venture into the unknown.

Key 77   Documentation

OVERVIEW   *Documentation is the written instructions provided with a computer program.*

Types of documentation:
- **Reference manuals** that contain complete information about the program, organized by subject.
- **Tutorials** for new users.
- **"Quick-start" tutorials** for users who have experience with similar programs and want to learn the details of this one quickly.
- **User's guides** explaining advanced features and techniques to more experienced users.
- **On-line help** available on the computer while the program is running.

Good documentation: To write good documentation, you must realize that you are **explaining things to a human being, not just recording facts on paper**. Successful documentation must not only answer the user's questions, but also convince the user in advance that it is going to do so.

Use of examples: When writing documentation, be sure to include plenty of **examples** so the user can check his understanding. Some users prefer to learn **inductively**, figuring out the whole system from a series of examples rather than by reading about abstract principles. With complex but well-designed software, inductive learning is especially appropriate.

Conciseness: Like all writing, documentation must be **concise** and **get to the point**.

Clarity: A common fault is to use words that have not been defined or leave it unclear what question is supposed to be answered by a particular chapter in the documentation.

Remember the reader: To avoid these problems, **visualize the human reader** (keeping track of what he or she knows) and **divide the documentation into short sections, each with a clear purpose**.

Key 78   Copyrights and patents

OVERVIEW   *Copyrights and patents are forms of legal protection for software.*

Copyrights: Copyright (the *right* to *copy*) is the exclusive legal right to make copies of a book, picture, or computer program. Copyright **protects the original author or publisher from loss of income**. If other people were allowed to distribute copies of my programs without paying me, I would not be able to make money programming.

How to copyright: To copyright a computer program in the United States, you need not register it with the Copyright Office. Just include a notice of the form "Copyright © 1990 John Doe" on the screen and distribution disk.

Protection: Copyright protects **only the author's exact words** (pictures, program code, etc.), **not the ideas expressed in them**. Writing another program similar to an existing one, but not copied from it, is not a violation of copyright. Courts have held that **duplicating a program's menus or user interface** can be a violation of copyright, even if the program itself is not copied.

Software licensing: A **software license** is an agreement allowing someone to use a copyrighted program. Normally, when you "buy software," you are buying the **right to use the program on one machine**.

Copy protection: The use of special kinds of disks to prevent users from copying a program—uncommon nowadays.

Shareware: Software that is distributed free but requires a payment directly to the author from users. Shareware is copyrighted and the payment is part of the software license.

Patents: A **patent**, unlike a copyright, **protects an idea** (an invention). For a long time the U. S. Patent Office refused to patent computer programs on the grounds that an algorithm is a mathematical discovery, not an invention. Recently, however, **a few algorithms and programs have been patented**. The present law is somewhat unclear.

Key 79   Working conditions and health hazards

OVERVIEW *The main health hazards from using computers are job stress, eyestrain, and backaches (and related problems). There is no convincing evidence of a radiation hazard from computers.*

Known health hazards from using computers:
- **Job stress.** Some jobs that involve computers are very stressful. Some people have to sit constantly at computer screens and respond instantly to information appearing there. Not surprisingly, these people experience severe stress. They are being **used as components in a computer system** as if they themselves were machines. Unlike a machine, a human being needs frequent breaks, changes of pace, exercise, and, most of all, the dignity that comes from having some control over the way the work is done.
- **Eyestrain** from blurry screens and glare. Eyestrain does not permanently harm the eyes, but it makes many people notice for the first time that their eyesight is not perfect. This makes them think that the computer has harmed their vision. Often, eyeglasses are not designed to focus at the distance of a computer screen.
- **Backaches** and other muscle, nerve, and joint problems from sitting too long in uncomfortable positions and from lack of exercise.

Radiation hazards?
- Computers **do not emit ionizing radiation (radioactivity)**.
- Some computer screens emit tiny amounts of **X-rays**, but this is much less than the background level naturally present in the environment.
- Computer screens emit some **ultraviolet (UV) light**, but ordinary sunlight contains much more.
- **ELF (extremely-low-frequency) radiation** from computer screens **(video display terminals, VDTs)** consists of a weak oscillating magnetic field. This is not "radiation" in the usual sense of the word. Very strong ELF fields appear to have produced birth defects in animals, but this has not been confirmed.

Key 80 Effect of computers on society

OVERVIEW *Almost all the effects of computers on society have been **unexpected or contrary to predictions**. Computers have not produced mass unemployment, dictatorial control, or other predicted problems.*

Employment: Computers **have not put people out of work** as some people predicted. Instead, computers **make the same workers more productive**. Industry adopts computers to raise production, not to get rid of employees. Computers themselves have created a tremendous number of new jobs.

Changes: Computerization *does* require **changes in the nature of the work**. Sales clerks now type numbers on keyboards instead of counting coins in metal boxes. Compare computers to automobiles. Nobody claims the automobile has created mass unemployment, but few people nowadays drive nails into horses' hooves.

Education: Computers **do not require all workers to be highly educated**. There is a big difference between using a computer and programming one. A hotel clerk who uses a computer to reserve rooms does not need any more education than a hotel clerk who does things the old way.

Politics: Computers **have not led to central control of society**. Thirty years ago, experts foresaw a world in which everyone would be highly dependent on a few powerful central computers. This has not happened. Personal computers have become a **powerful force for democracy**. Computers communicate through **decentralized networks** that no single person can control. The pro-democracy uprising in China in 1989 was made possible partly by information traveling on computer networks, thereby avoiding government censorship.

Remaining problems

Misconceptions: One continuing problem is that **people tend to think everything that a computer says must be true.**
* In the 1960s, many of us heard our creditors say, "According to our computer, you owe us money," as if the computer were automatically right.
* In 1990, a Georgia driver is reported to have spent the night in jail because a South Carolina computer, using a database from the wrong year, said his license plate number belonged to a stolen car.

Privacy: Another concern is **misuse of personal data**.

- People give lots of personal information to banks, creditors, schools, etc., assuming the information will not travel very far. Nowadays, almost all this information is in computers.
- If all these databases were combined and cross-referenced automatically, the information could be used in ways that the people never foresaw when they gave it out. In effect, this would be an **invasion of privacy**.
- What's worse, any **false information** in the database could haunt people for a long time and be nearly impossible to correct.

GLOSSARY

algorithm
A precise procedure for doing a computation. An algorithm must say exactly what is to be done at each step, and it must always finish after a finite number of steps.

array
A data structure in which all elements are of the same type and are identified by number (e.g., $x[1]$, $x[2]$ ... $x[99]$).

assembly language
A programming language consisting of simple abbreviations for machine instructions (machine code).

bit
The amount of information represented by a single "on" or "off," "true" or "false," or "0" or "1" signal.

bootstrapping (booting)
Starting up a computer by running a program that makes it load and run another program, "pulling itself up by its bootstraps."

bus
The system of parallel wires or connections that join the CPU, memory, and other parts of a computer.

byte
A group of eight bits; enough information to represent one printed character.

compiler
A program that automatically translates programs from a language such as Pascal or C into machine language so that the computer can run them.

CPU
The central processing unit of a computer, where all computation is carried out.

data structures
Ways of arranging data in a computer program, including arrays, records, and lists.

diskette
A disk (flexible or rigid) that can be removed easily from the computer.

floppy disk A flexible disk that can be removed easily from the computer. Floppy disks are now usually called diskettes.

hard disk A disk drive permanently mounted in a machine.

heuristic A procedure that does not always solve a problem, but usually produces the correct answer or a good approximation quickly.

kilobyte (K) 1024 bytes. (Not 1000, because $1024 = 2^{10}$.)

list A data structure in which each element is stored with a pointer to the next one. Elements can be inserted into the list by rearranging pointers, without moving the elements that are already there.

load To copy a program from some other source into memory, making it possible for the computer to run the program.

machine language (machine code) The internal binary code that controls the CPU. Programs are normally written in other languages and translated into machine language by a compiler.

mainframe 1. The largest kind of computer, big enough to fill a room or several rooms. 2. The main cabinet where the CPU of a mainframe computer is housed.

megabyte 1,048,576 bytes. (Not 1,000,000, because $1,048,576 = 2^{20}$.)

memory The part of a computer where information and programs are held while the program is actually running. The term "memory" includes RAM and ROM but does not normally include disks or tapes.

microcomputer A computer whose CPU is a microprocessor.

microprocessor A CPU built on a single silicon chip (integrated circuit).

minicomputer   A computer whose CPU is larger than a microprocessor, but small enough to fit on one or two circuit boards.

NP-complete   As difficult as any problem in the set NP, such as the traveling salesman problem. NP-complete problems require impossibly large amounts of computer time to solve.

operating system   The program that controls the overall operation of a computer and enables it to run other programs.

pointer   A variable that contains the location of another variable.

RAM   Random-access memory; the type of memory in which computers normally hold programs and data while working on them.

record   A data structure in which elements can be of different types are are identified by name (for example, `stu-dent.name`, `student.class`, `stu-dent.average`).

ROM   Read-only memory; memory containing important programs (such as part of the operating system) permanently recorded.

semantics   The rules of a programming language (or a human language) that specify what the words or symbols mean.

supercomputer   A large computer that uses unconventional design to obtain very high speed.

syntax   The rules of a programming language (or a human language) that specify how symbols are put together. For example, Pascal syntax requires semicolons between statements.

variable   A named location in which a value can be stored, such as X in the statement LET X=2.

INDEX